THE Rest

REVOLUTION

AMANDA MILLER LITTLEJOHN

THE
Rest
REVOLUTION

How to Reclaim Your Rhythm and Conquer Burnout
When **Overworking** Has Become the Norm

WILEY

Published by John Wiley & Sons, Inc., Hoboken, New Jersey.
Published simultaneously in Canada.

For general information on our other products and services or for technical support, please contact our Customer Care Department within the United States at (800) 762-2974, outside the United States at (317) 572-3993 or fax (317) 572-4002.

Wiley also publishes its books in a variety of electronic formats. Some content that appears in print may not be available in electronic formats. For more information about Wiley products, visit our web site at www.wiley.com.

Library of Congress Cataloging-in-Publication Data Is Available:

ISBN 9781394259106 (Cloth)
ISBN 9781394259113 (ePub)
ISBN 9781394259120 (ePDF)

Cover Design: Wiley
Cover Images: © AndrewD/Adobe Stock, © malshak_off/Adobe Stock
Author Photo: © Danielle Finney
SKY10085550_092024

I dedicate this book to my mother, Mattie Pearl Sevier Miller.
Thank you for planting the seed of this idea long before
I got here, having the strength to keep going through
burnout, and modeling the art of restoration through the many
seasons of your life. Merci, Mama!

Contents

Preface

We are in the middle of a Rest Revolution.

The pandemic was a wake-up call for work. Americans finally recognized how utterly exhausted we all were, how our modern work habits were unsustainable, and how overworking had become our religion. We collectively saw the insanity in our days, where our priorities were in the wrong places, and where we needed to make corrections. We asked ourselves the tough questions, and some downgraded lifestyles to make more time and space to enjoy our hobbies, our loved ones, and our lives.

For a time, employers stepped up and affirmed worker calls to prioritize well-being by creating employee wellness programming and inclusion efforts that honored the whole person.

With many offices closed, remote work – formerly an outlier – became the only way most of us were working. And we all found out that it works. But as more and more employers move past the post-pandemic cocoons, we have found ourselves at an inflection point.

The pandemic offered many employees the rare opportunity to shift the paradigm of work. The window may be closing, but it is not closed yet. We can still push; we can still fight to maintain the progress we've worked so hard for.

It's time for a rest revolution that shifts our approach to work, and this book is my reporting from the front lines.

Many have come to the realization that working twice as hard never yielded enough to make it worth the effort. Those who have prized their work ethic and their ability to power through in the past are reconsidering whether that's something to be proud of. On the heels of a global pandemic, many are beginning to view their grandparents' and parents' relationship to hard work for what it was – a byproduct of the times, a result of social conditioning, and the residue of immigrant values and/or slavery mindset – instead of the gospel truth.

I am not an expert on rest. Somewhat by default, my identity as a Black woman reared in the South makes me an expert on over-working. My identity as a woman and having been socialized as such makes me a bit of an expert on perfectionism. And my identity as a mother who is rearing three children makes me an expert on exhaustion, overachieving, and ineffective multitasking.

My point here is that I am not a doctor or a mental health expert. And, unless you consider yourself one of the seven million medical professionals roaming this planet, neither are you. We likely have similar journeys, and you will likely relate to some of the experiences I've had, and the experiences that the folks I'll be sharing with you in this book have had as well.

I have spoken to a number of experts to get the scientific point of view. But I want to set your expectations and let you know I am not qualified to advise you on your physical and mental health.

Now that I've gotten that disclaimer out of the way, I will say what I *am* an expert in. I am an expert pattern-seer and formula finder. I am a highly sensitive person, so I notice subtle changes around me, such as when I realized there were fewer birds singing in the forest than the previous week. I shared this observance with my kids – where are all the birds going?

Due to my sensitivity and through my own personal journey and my journaling, I often find myself capturing a sense of what we are all going through but may not have the words to articulate. I have been journaling consistently for the majority of my life, so that daily practice, combined with my keen observation skills, and knack for spotting subtle changes in my environment, does make me the expert to write this book.

Like many of you, I began to notice a recurring story in my social media feeds, and even in my conversations with fellow moms, both during and immediately after the pandemic. Suddenly, everyone was taking a break, taking a sabbatical, stepping away from social media, giving up things they had previously felt compelled to make room for. The pandemic showed so many of us where we just didn't have the room. At first it seemed like a fluke. It began with people giving up social media, then giving up their job, then quelling their ambition, and even lowering their earning goals. It seemed to be a similar pattern that was playing out for me as well.

After having my third child during the pandemic, I had very limited social support – my mom didn't even come to meet the baby until she was six months old. (By comparison, my mother was in the hospital waiting room and was the first person to hold both of my other babies after my husband and me.)

But after having my third child, I had a personal reckoning. What was I working so hard for, what did it all mean, and what messages was I passing down to my children? Burnout is real and I experienced it firsthand. Before that, I had yet to meet my limit, but now here I was.

Introduction: My Burnout Story

My Silent Addiction

My name is Amanda, and I'm an addict.

For the past 30 years, I've been struggling with a dangerous and silent addiction to overworking. And for 20 years, I don't think I even knew that's what it was.

I didn't recognize it because this addiction helped me to get things that made me feel good about myself. This addiction helped me attract attention and make my parents, spouse, and ultimately my children proud.

Overworking, overperforming, and overachieving served me well for a long time. That is, until I had a newborn baby, and also found myself at home with traumatized remote-schooling teens, evading a deadly virus, and managing a business that was bursting at the seams, all during a global pandemic.

My chronic overworking – coupled with sleep-deprived new mom moments – reached a point of burnout so severe that I cycled in and out of depression, became prone to infections, and my body began breaking down. But hey, the bank account was overflowing and clients were getting great results.

And honestly, despite my health challenges and physical exhaustion, I probably would have kept overworking had my teenagers not been present to witness and hold a mirror up to my insanity.

A Wake-up Call

By mid-pandemic, I had a new infant, two teens, and a business that was overflowing. Between working from home and schooling from home, there was always something happening in the house and it seemed like things were always falling through the cracks.

One very early Monday morning, I remember trying without success to shake off the grogginess when I rose to get some work done while the rest of the house slept. It was 3 a.m., and I had a full day of Zoom meetings before me and no other time to prepare. But by 6 a.m. I was mentally slogging through my work and feeling warm. By the time I'd thought to take my temperature I was burning up. I retrieved the steaming thermometer I'd tucked under my tongue and read the big red digital numbers: 101.5.

"Great," I thought. Behind on a few of my deliverables and already overdue for nursing my one-month-old daughter, I had no time to be sick.

The day before I'd noticed shooting pains piercing my right breast and I'd attempted to schedule a telemedicine appointment. When I finally got through and saw the doctor pop up on my iPhone screen, my fever had reached 103.5 and I was listless, lying in a pool of my own sweat.

This particular episode was precipitated by having a baby just a month earlier and recovering from a difficult cesarean surgery while still working. And because I had a newborn, my sleep schedule was out of whack, so I was up at all hours of the night trying to squeeze in work whenever I had a chance. Weakened by the trauma of surgery and sleep deprivation, my body decided to shut the whole thing down.

Halfway on the other side, I thought my experience had been largely my own. I had soldiered through a painful breast infection that sadly ended my nursing journey prematurely. No matter how groggy and disoriented, I nevertheless kept showing up on Zoom. I hadn't considered how that episode had impacted my kids, until they spoke up about it.

My son Logan, then in the ninth grade, told me that watching me fall sick from overworking made him anxious. "Your body was giving you clear signs you need to rest and you were just ignoring them," he said. "It was like watching you spiral downhill."

Connor, an eighth grader at the time, had tended to me between virtual classes on Zoom when my fever was at its height. He later told me it frightened him to see me that way.

I felt a mix of emotions upon hearing that from my kids. I was embarrassed, ashamed, disappointed. I prided myself on putting them first, healing my wounds so as not to pass them on and learning new tools to give them what I thought would amount to a great start in life. Had I just negated all of that by pulling back the curtain to who I *really* was and how I *really* operated when they were usually blissfully unaware at school?

My slip was hanging, as my grandmother used to say.

A Dangerous Example

To hear that my behavior was not only setting a dangerous model for my children but was scaring them was a wake-up call. It was one thing to put myself in danger, and another thing entirely to scare the kids. (I know – put your own mask on first.) Plus, I didn't want my kids to interpret my behavior as the acceptable way to do things. I knew I had to do something different.

But as it turns out, the pandemic put a lot of parents' and kids' unsustainable approaches to work front and center.

Kristian Owens, a therapist who treats children in the DC area, said that at the height of the pandemic she saw not only kids who were struggling, but parents who were chronically exhausted, emotionally distant, and downright disconnected.

Owens told me that burnout doesn't impact only adults. When parents are burned out, that prevents them from being emotionally present for their children, and when the kids pick up on this distance, it can lead to a host of mental and emotional problems.

The pandemic only turbocharged these issues. Owens's small practice swelled during the pandemic as frantic parents sought mental health services for their children. "Their children were being impacted from the isolation, from being away from their friends and having to do virtual school, but also because parents were not being emotionally present because they were also burned out."

With so many school-age kids home during some part of the COVID-19 pandemic, it was unfortunately not uncommon for kids to witness parental burnout. "If you're working in a work environment that is stressful and then you're coming home and you're having to parent, it's like, I don't have it to give, I'm so exhausted from my day," Owens explained. "And then I'm coming home and, especially as a mom with all the hats we wear, I can't be emotionally present because I'm not even emotionally present for myself."

One morning over coffee, I got the wake-up call I didn't know I needed. I was planning to take a sabbatical from work and was telling my teenaged son about my plans. He was happy to hear that I was finally intentionally taking a break. Reflecting on this season of overworking, he expressed his experience of watching me spiral out while virtual schooling from home.

"Did you see yourself earlier this year?" he asked me. "You were staying up all night. You were limping around in pain. You were irritated and seemed sad. You were always busy and never had time to talk."

Hearing his account was eye-opening, and a bit painful, but I asked him to go on.

"It was hard to be around you," he said finally. "It made me sad." Ouch.

While my sons were able to describe their emotional experience of watching me struggle, that's rare for most kids. Instead of telling you how they feel, most kids simply act out. But whether they talk to you like my sons did or resort to temper tantrums, according to Owens kids are still picking up on more than we realize. And instead of speaking up they may try to get our attention by acting out at home or school.

Jalan Burton, MD, is a pediatrician with a mobile practice (she was also my pediatrician who made home visits to my baby during the pandemic). Instead of having patients come to an office to see her, she travels to her patients' homes, and in 2020 and 2021, she got an eyeful. She saw more depression, anxiety, and irritability with parents. She ordinarily administers initial depression screenings for mothers of newborns in the baby's first few months of life, but given the symptoms she was observing during routine visits, she had to increase her frequency.

"I found I was having to do it more often because parents were so burned out," she explained. When parents weren't following up with mental health professionals despite indicating depression, anxiety, and irritability during those screenings, she began asking if they wanted her to reach out to a therapist on their behalf to get the ball rolling. "Every single person I said that to took me up on the offer," she said.

Dropping Like Flies Emotionally

Owens found that during the pandemic, schools were still expecting kids to show up like we weren't in a global pandemic and experiencing this collective trauma. As she put it, "Kids were like dropping like flies emotionally."

And while parental ambition is somewhat to blame, in her opinion, our society pushes everyone to overwork. "We have been indoctrinated by a society that perpetuates grind, grind, grind, so it makes sense that's what we've been teaching our kids," she said.

And that grind comes at a cost. For me, it came at the cost of my physical and mental health. But it can be even more damaging for young people who aren't emotionally equipped to deal with the fallout.

In the Washington, DC, area where I live, ambitions run high. But apparently so do the negative effects. "I see so many kids who are getting straight A's, they go to the top schools in this area, and they're so emotionally unhealthy," Owens told me. Many of her teen patients struggle with depression and make it to the end of high school with great grades, only to stall out early in college because they're already burnt out from having to maintain so much academically.

The Match That Lit Our Collective Burnout

The pandemic didn't cause the fire of burnout, but it certainly lit a match.

According to McKinsey, burnout is defined as "the feeling of depletion, cynicism, and emotional distance that results from a lack of impact or autonomy at work." That likely sounds familiar to you if you consider yourself ambitious, a high achiever, a go-getter, or any number of monikers that suggest upward mobility.

But high achiever or not, the pandemic fostered widespread burnout for several reasons. With lives on the line, the pandemic created an increased workload and pressure for many people, especially in the healthcare fields. Essential workers faced overwhelming patient loads and long hours when the pandemic was at its height. This constant strain led to exhaustion and a feeling of never being able to catch up.

Remote work became the norm for many, and the lines between professional and personal life became hazy. Those work-life boundaries got very blurry. People found themselves constantly available, working longer hours, and struggling to disconnect. On top of this, quarantining created social isolation and widespread loneliness. Most people were forced to create new routines.

It was such an uncertain time and we were in constant fear for our lives, especially prior to the introduction of a vaccine. I remember staying glued to the news waiting for Dr. Fauci's latest guidance. I had never watched so much news before, and as many others experienced, the constant barrage of news about the pandemic, coupled with the fear of getting sick or losing loved ones, fueled anxiety and stress.

These factors combined to create a perfect storm for widespread burnout during the COVID-19 pandemic. But as with my own lifetime of overworking, our collective problems started long before 2020.

1 | Roots of Machine Mindset

During the late 1800s, immigrants and African Americans – many newly freed slaves – sought work in the rising industrial America. As the railroad industry evolved, the need grew for laborers to build new transportation infrastructure – particularly on the railroads that were connecting the coastal cities with the rest of the country.

As legend has it – and some would say the story is rooted in real history – an African American man by the name of John Henry earned a reputation as the strongest and fastest steel driver working on the railroads. Steel drivers were responsible for manually hammering a drill through the hard rock of a mountain bed so that explosives could later be placed in the holes. This enabled incremental parts of the mountain to be blasted away, making room for train tracks and tunnels.

John Henry was hired in West Virginia to help work on Great Bend – a 6,450-foot-long tunnel through Big Bend Mountain. Imagine drilling and blasting your way through a mountain – this was slow, tedious, and exhausting work.

Two years in, C&O Canal executives brought in the newly invented steam-powered drill to help speed up the process. The steam drill was reportedly able to drill faster than any man, and for John Henry, whose reputation was built on his speed and power, the challenge was on.

John Henry went to work against the steam drill, hammering into the mountain rock. At one point, he's said to have held a 10-pound hammer in each hand as he pounded his manual drill into the mountain while the steam drill did the same. It's said that John Henry drilled a 14-foot hole into the rock, besting the machine, which only drilled 9 feet. Victorious, he completed the race and dropped dead from overexertion.

John Henry maintained his reputation as the strongest, fastest man working on the railroad, but it came at the price of his very life.

Self-Work as Worth and Validation

Although the story of John Henry sits in the realm of legend, it's nevertheless a powerful illustration of our modern beliefs about work and can provide clues to how those beliefs evolved.

Whether you believe this folktale is purely fictional or inspired by true events, as a symbol John Henry provides a powerful illustration of how American esteem and identity has been linked to work. To me, it speaks to the natural human reaction and desire to hold on to the past when innovation potentially threatens one's livelihood. It's the natural human reaction, but ultimately, instead of pitting yourself against something with which you cannot compete, just find a different way to make your mark.

John Henry's identity was so tied to being the fastest and strongest in his field that a new technology that would have likely made his job easier instead wound up threatening his sense of self.

This is understandable. He spent his adult life – newly freed from slavery, no less – becoming the best and fastest in his field. And here comes this machine that doesn't require breaks, doesn't need to eat, and in fact doesn't do much of anything, and yet can outwork someone who has spent much of their adult life – and built their entire reputation and identity – around being able to do this thing this way, this fast, this well. Here's a machine that made someone's achievements obsolete in an instant.

Even so, John Henry surmised that if he could just work harder, he could outwork becoming obsolete.

From our present-day vantage point, I think we'd all agree that is the wrong approach. To ignore the changes in a system, or in the environment, or yourself – and do what you've always done, just harder, longer, faster, more, more, more – simply doesn't work.

Like John Henry, we're human beings, not machines, yet we're approaching the demands of work as if we are. Machines like the steam drill may not need to eat, sleep, or restore themselves, but human beings do.

In many workplaces, fast-paced environments are designed with the expectation that human beings will produce machine-level outputs: better, cheaper, faster, more.

Ultimately, once you understand that, you must ask yourself this: are you willing to die for this arbitrary outcome? Are you going to operate as a machine, or will you reclaim your humanity?

From machine to being – *that* is the future of work. That is a challenge worthy of our time and attention. How can you resolve to remember your humanity, and honor it while doing the work you do?

My Connection

I can relate wholeheartedly to the validation and identity John Henry derived from overworking.

For me, the problem began as early as elementary school when I realized that a beautiful string of A's made my parents beam. As their marriage fell apart and they hurled hurtful words at each other, I think I was subconsciously willing to do anything I could to break the tension. If that meant straight A's, Junior Honor Society inductions, AP classes, and National Merit Scholarships, so be it.

And perfect grades were just the beginning. As any good achiever knows, as you advance in the workplace, there are many chances to make your mark if you're looking for opportunities to do so. High standards, talent, and opportunity became a dangerous mix for me as I pushed myself to attain more and more.

Even more complicated was that my stamina to work harder than others were willing to and my ability to suss out an opportunity to achieve proved to be more than a career asset. It proved to be the basis of a powerful framework that has helped hundreds of others quickly determine where they are already getting traction, and where they can exploit that for even more traction in the field of their choosing.

I'm proud of that – really, really proud of that. But I have come to realize that, like John Henry's winning nail spike, it was not without a price.

A Psychological Perspective

Dr. Reisha Moxley is a psychologist who works primarily with high-achieving professionals. She says the root of overworking can be traced in this country to work's status as many people's primary source of validation.

"If you are dissatisfied and/or longing for deeper connection elsewhere, work can serve as a distraction and provide needed dopamine hits when they are scarce in our nonwork lives," she told me.

Ouch. I'm definitely guilty of using work to avoid things I'd rather not deal with.

But Moxley says an individual's identity, esteem, and sense of worth can all easily get tangled up in their work because boundaries get hazy. Especially if the individual is getting validation, however complicated, from their work identity, that work identity can eclipse everything.

"It may be the only place they are consistently rewarded (pay, promotions, benefits) in their lives," Moxley said.

Creating a Social Norm

While concerns on the individual level can influence a person's desire to overwork, modern day ideas about work helped to get us here.

The roots of overwork can undeniably be traced further back, but I want to go back about 150 years to the height of the American Industrial Revolution. The rise of industrial America was a period after the Civil War that transformed American society, including mindsets and attitudes about work.

During this period of rapid change, Americans began replacing manual labor – like John Henry's man-powered hammer and drill – with machine labor that sped up production. The wider availability of water power, steam power, and later electricity helped to speed up processes and production. Workers moved from farms to factories as our agriculture-driven economy gave way to manufacturing. Our society became more connected as railways, canals, and the like created faster ways to move goods and people.

All of these changes – in machine innovation, power, and transportation – meant that demand for labor increased significantly. So did the promise of economic opportunity.

Beginnings of Labor

America quickly earned a reputation for being a land of opportunity – a place where, unless you were African American, you had the chance to make something of yourself. In Europe, for example, upward mobility was (and often still is) fairly uncommon. Whatever social class or "caste" you were born into is where you stayed.

But in America, you weren't confined to your caste or station of birth.

As steam power, water power, and new machinery improved production, they created a demand for labor. More labor and machinery created a surplus of products to sell, and this surplus created a demand for new ways to transport goods and move people around.

Building a new society and the transportation to connect us – roads, railroads, tunnels, canals, bridges – created opportunity. But it came at a human cost.

Around this time, poor immigrants from Europe came to the United States looking for economic opportunity, and to escape religious persecution. Most became city dwellers because they didn't have the resources to move around and had to settle in the cities in which the ships landed. They often worked very low-wage roles and settled for dangerous work.

For instance, 1,000 of 50,000 workers died during the construction of the Erie Canal that ran between the Hudson River in New York and Lake Erie. At least 764 workers died within five years of completing the 3-mile Hawks Nest Tunnel through a West Virginia mountain, primarily from breathing silica dust, though some estimates put the death toll over 2,000.

But the promise of a better life – and the idea that by working hard one can create a whole new life in America – was difficult to resist. Hard work was the key to survival, and it held the promise of upward mobility. For the sons and daughters of European immigrants, it's easy to see how hard work could become a value passed down through the generations.

For African Americans after emancipation, work for pay was a revolution. Before then many Blacks had toiled in unpaid servitude in the South – bought and sold as if they *were* machines, and often discarded when they were no longer of economic use.

Many Black Americans like myself can trace the overworking mindset back to these newly freed slaves who had been bought and sold for their labor. Their identities and value in society therefore were directly linked to the work they produced.

Rise of Sociological Ideas

Around the same time, Frederick Taylor, a mechanical engineer, watched as steam and water power revolutionized the American labor force. As work moved from farms to factories and transformed workforces from family units to buildings full of strangers, new dilemmas emerged. Taylor wondered, *How will we organize all of this work and manage all of these people?*

An easy way, Taylor decided, was to streamline, systemize, and standardize work. Through his powerful "time and motion studies," he observed and timed tasks to analyze work efficiency before advising companies on how to increase productivity. He would determine how workers could spend the least amount of time completing their tasks in the fewest movements.

Using his background as a mechanical engineer, he came up with the most efficient pathway to complete tasks through detailed time and motion studies. For example, he experimented with shovels of different weights and sizes and found that a shovel weighing around 21 pounds was perfect for moving material without tiring out the worker. This simple change led to huge productivity boosts, especially in tasks like coal shoveling.

Another experiment of Taylor's involved bricklaying. He watched bricklayers closely and analyzed every single movement they made. By tweaking their movements and tools, he came up with a new method that cut out unnecessary steps. His optimized process included positioning the bricks and mortar at waist height, so workers didn't have to bend down as much, and standardizing how bricks were picked up and laid. This new technique allowed bricklayers to go from laying about 1,000 bricks a day to over 2,700.

Taylor's innovations in shovel design and bricklaying are just two examples of how his time and motion studies transformed industrial efficiency and set the stage for modern practices in manufacturing and labor management. His work led to productivity increases of 200–400%.

But he did it by essentially engineering new ways for humans to produce and operate uniformly, efficiently, and reliably – much like machines.

Taylor's experiments with worker efficiency established the field of study that would later become known as "Taylorism" or "scientific management." Sold on the increased production made possible by his efficiencies, companies adopted his methods, further cementing machine-level expectations from humans.

Systemic Threats

Around the same time Taylor was conducting his time and motion studies, German sociologist Max Weber was pondering how moving from small family-run farms and shops would impact how organizations assigned tasks, evaluated performance, and rewarded talent.

Dubbed the father of bureaucracy, Weber advocated for formal rules and policies that would protect workers from favoritism stemming from family ties and alliances based on shared race, religious affiliation, or nationality. This favoritism, which he called particularism, could set up different groups of workers to be judged by differing yardsticks.

As it turns out, this particularism or "similarity bias" in today's language can be an exhausting phenomenon to navigate at work – that is, when it's not working in your favor.

Amber Cabral is in many ways furthering Weber's work. In her leadership and workplace culture consulting, she's seen firsthand how unchecked particularism can create unnecessary labor for those without the favoritism of leaders in the workplace and compound the type of exhaustion that eventually leads to burnout.

As an award-winning consultant, speaker, and trainer, Cabral travels almost weekly for work. She also uses her identity of being gluten-free to illustrate the additional labor created by navigating a world that wasn't designed with your differences in mind. She considers being gluten-free an identity matter. Most identity matters that are less common create additional labor for the person who's experiencing them.

"I'm a gluten-free person who has been to a lot of conferences, has been asked to speak at a lot of conferences, who's been invited to a lot of shared events or activity spaces," she told me. "And what happens constantly is that I have to make a decision that I'm either going to be willing to teach everybody about gluten-free today and navigate the discomfort, or I'm going to choose not to eat."

She shared how although she regularly makes a point to note her dietary restrictions beforehand, invariably conference organizers will overlook her request for a gluten-free meal. Then she'll be offered a meal that she has to return, explain her previous request, and wait for an alternative. In the meantime, she's often peppered with questions from her tablemates as to why she isn't eating, which launches a discussion about her identity when all she wanted to do was have a meal.

"So now I've got to give a lesson on what gluten-free means. And invariably, someone else at the table is one of those folks who thinks that gluten-free is real only if you have celiac disease. So now I've got to explain that I've been tested and I have celiac disease. So now I'm actually teaching a lesson instead of eating." Eventually Cabral says, her food arrives, but it's usually once everyone else is already done eating. And the meal is generally a hodgepodge of items instead of a true meal.

When you take the example of navigating the world as a gluten-free individual, you can see how the labor involved can begin to compound over time. When you must mentally make a note of your options or come prepared with your own food when traveling, the extra work on top of regular work adds up.

The fewer identity privileges you have, the more labor you have to do, and the more at risk you are for burnout when work demands rise because matters of identity create work for the people who are experiencing them.

We all have visible and invisible identities – we may be gluten-free, neurodivergent, or some other identity. We may speak with a heavy accent or wear a hijab to work. When your identity falls outside of what society deems the norm, the more labor you have to do on top of your actual job duties. That labor compounds and can add to burnout.

In fact, according to the Society for Human Resource Management, identity played a major role in employees' comfort with remote work during the pandemic. Many Black employees preferred remote work during that time because it lessened their experiences of race-based microaggressions. A survey by research firm Future Forum revealed that only 3% of Black white-collar employees wanted to return to in-person work, compared to 21% of their white counterparts.

A Series of Misalignments

As defined by the World Health Organization, "Burn-out is a syndrome conceptualized as resulting from chronic workplace stress that has not been successfully managed." It is characterized by three dimensions:

- Feelings of energy depletion or exhaustion
- Increased mental distance from one's job, or feelings of negativism or cynicism related to one's job
- Reduced professional efficacy

"Burn-out refers specifically to phenomena in the occupational context and should not be applied to describe experiences in other areas of life."

But despite the WHO definition, which frames burnout as an individual problem that has not been successfully managed by the individual, systemic issues contribute to the experience of employees in the workplace.

The premise of this book is basically that burnout is caused by a series of misalignments. These misalignments go against our natural inclinations, creating friction that leads to energy leaks. As these energy leaks compound, we experience a sense of burnout brought on by having to account for so much friction.

In addition, since we are not allowing ourselves access to the things that generate energy for us – the aligned things – we miss out on the chance to naturally fuel our tanks. But by reducing the friction of misalignment and allowing ourselves to partake in the energy-generating activities, work, and relationships that are unique to us, we will generate the energy we need to exit burnout.

2
Overworking on Autopilot

One of the ways machine mindset keeps us misaligned is via the practice of overworking on autopilot. This refers to the muscle memory that develops as a result of habitual overwork. It includes the act of pushing through and ignoring one's physical and emotional needs after a major health event, life crisis, death, or trauma.

Overworking on autopilot is characterized by five key beliefs:

1. I have to be perfect to be worthy.
2. I overachieve, therefore I am – achieving is not enough; I have to work twice as hard.
3. I have to push through my physical or emotional pain.
4. My worth is tied to my labor and ability to produce.
5. I didn't truly earn my success (imposter syndrome).

Perfectionism

One of the beliefs that undergirds overworking on autopilot is the belief that we must be perfect to be worthy. According to journalist

L'Oreal Thompson Payton, author of *Stop Waiting to Be Perfect*, perfectionism is a dangerous cocktail of constantly trying to over-work, overachieve, and prove yourself, often to the detriment of your own mental health and well-being.

"I was the straight-A student, I was the valedictorian, I was on the honor roll, I had literal perfect attendance, awards, and it all comes at a cost," Thompson told me. "Sure, it paves the way for success. I wouldn't be sitting here talking to you now, probably, if it were not for a lot of those perfectionist tendencies.

"The downside is how it can become all-consuming and really take a toll on not even just your mental health, but your physical health as well."

Payton says her perfectionism was largely a beast of her own making. She doesn't recall her parents insisting on straight A's. "I think I was just naturally smart." She loved to learn, loved school, and academics came easily to her. But somewhere along the way, perfection became the standard she set for herself. She told herself she always had to earn the A and be the best to be worthy.

And it didn't stop with getting the grades and being the best at school. "It was interesting because there aren't gold stars in the real world essentially, but they do come in the form of awards and as a jour-nalist in my first job out of the gate I won an award from a regional press association, and so the perfectionism continued."

Payton said the pandemic coupled with a very arduous fertility journey caused her to double down on what she could control in her life. She channeled her perfectionist tendencies into her Peloton streak, which she held for more than 600 days, until one day she missed a workout and the streak ended.

"And when I lost it, I literally cried. But that was really a wake-up moment for me because I realized my self-worth. I'm still L'Oreal, I'm still worthy of love and dignity. Like every good thing in this world, my self-worth is not tied up in this streak."

Payton said for her, her perfectionism led to burnout. Years of always trying to be the best, always going after the promotion, constantly overworking, and going above and beyond in the workplace all took its toll. She believed that if she did a good job, showed up, and did the work, she would finally feel worthy. But self-worth is an inside job that isn't impacted by perfect performance reviews.

Groomed to Overachieve and Work Twice as Hard

Confronting one's ideas about working hard versus deserving rest can be life-changing and perspective-challenging. I have believed that being a "hard worker" was a personality trait, a value, and key to my success for most of my life. I am now revisiting this idea and challenging it. Do I *have* to work hard to have success? Does it have to be difficult in order to mean I'm doing a good job? Can it just be easy? Don't I deserve some downtime?

Children who were not born independently wealthy in the 1960s, 1970s, 1980s, and even as late as the 1990s often report a common message that came from their parents in those early years: "You have to work twice as hard to get half as much in this world."

Particularly for the working class, immigrants, and people of color, this mantra became a shorthand to explain an American work ethic rooted in the idea that success was tenuous, fragile, and had to be wrestled to the ground by brute strength.

But driving oneself to exert 200% effort is unsustainable and over time can lead to the burnout that so many are collectively experiencing. "We have been groomed to overachieve," said Amber Cabral of high achievers – specifically Black women in high-profile roles who've had to overcome systemic barriers to get ahead. "We know how to boss up and get it done. So it's about reprogramming the idea that it's weak to say you can't do more."

When you're groomed to overachieve – when mere achievement is not enough – and you're trained to work twice as hard to be deemed good enough, the stage is set for overworking. You've created a habitual approach to work that develops its own muscle memory. It becomes the default approach to work and can seamlessly flow into overworking on autopilot.

For overachievers, the idea that a strong work ethic is the most important tool one has to reach one's goals has been passed down as gospel. "Work twice as hard" is well-circulated counsel that has been passed down through generations and widely accepted as good advice.

But in fact, this is simply a long-held social norm that's just not true.

Pushing Through Physical or Emotional Pain

Several months ago, I reached out to a client prospect – let's call her Jennifer – who'd been given my name by the friend of a previous coaching client. Because this connection was three degrees away, Jennifer had to be reminded by her boss (a friend of the client who had referred me) to make the meeting happen. But make it happen she did, and after a few rounds of email tag we were scheduled for an 11 a.m. Zoom meeting.

I hopped on the Zoom promptly at 11 a.m. to find Jennifer staring back at me from her seat in an empty conference room. She was dressed conservatively in a black suit and stared back with a poker face, so I opened up with a joke and attempted to break the ice. When I asked Jennifer how she was doing, she waffled a bit before disclosing the truth that she'd had a rough morning. A mentor of hers had passed away a few hours ago and she along with others from her network were reeling from the news. As she tried to focus on our meeting, her phone began to ping with messages from others in her network who were checking in with her and processing their mentor's sudden passing.

I searched Jennifer's face intently. Though she was buttoned up and professional, it was obvious to me that her mentor had meant a lot to her. "I was just with her the other night. I visited her in the hospital," she told me as she held herself together.

At that point, I asked Jennifer if she'd rather reschedule our call for another time. She declined, saying we had the time blocked off and she was available to focus on how we could potentially work together. But her phone kept pinging.

"You know what, this conversation is not urgent. It will hold," I told Jennifer. "Why don't I just give you these 30 minutes back so you can get back to your friends and you all can begin to process this loss?"

Initially, she declined, again saying it had taken us a while to get the call on the calendar. But after 10 seconds or so I saw her take a deep breath and I watched her shoulders drop. It was as if a switch went off as her machine mind switched off and her humanity stepped forward. Her face softened.

"I think I'm going to take you up on that," she said. "Thank you."

Jennifer's story, while a simple example, is a perfect illustration of overworking on autopilot and how a deeply entrenched machine mindset can convince us that nothing is more important than keeping a work commitment.

Jennifer would rather have kept a 30-minute appointment with a stranger for the sake of not being perceived as unreliable or flaky than acknowledge her very real and valid human need to remove herself from work tasks for at least a few hours as she figured out how to process this tremendous personal loss.

Sadly, one of the recurring refrains I heard while interviewing people for this book was how a lack of time to grieve a major personal loss often led to a burnout breaking point that forced them to change their approach to work. But we'll get to that in Chapter 5.

Work, Labor, and Ability to Produce Equated with Worth

Dr. Adia Gooden is a clinical psychologist who helps high-achieving professionals move past what she terms "conditional self-worth" – the idea that one will be worthy when they do or have something outside of themselves. She's seen this sense of conditional self-worth increasingly push women to equate their worth with the quality of their work, judge themselves by how much they can work, or only consider themselves of value when they are working.

Low feelings of self-worth can lead to overwork, which can lead to burnout – and this cycle generally starts at an early age.

"I think often the people who are overworking were the high-achieving Type A, straight A students who were really praised and affirmed for doing the most," Gooden said. "We can sort of be socialized into that tendency from a very young age."

When it comes to each individual's predisposition to overworking, Gooden says that biases and discrimination can play a huge role on our experiences. When we internalize those workplace biases and discrimination, we feed feelings of conditional self-worth, which can then lead to overworking to feel worthy, and eventually to burnout.

"It can feel sort of like, well, if I just outperform, outshine, overwork, then I'm going to overcome feelings of low self-worth or I'm going to overcome biases against me because of my identity," Gooden said. "A combination of those things can set us up to overwork."

Imposter Syndrome: I Didn't Truly Earn My Success

First identified in 1978 by psychologists Dr. Clance and Dr. Imes, imposter syndrome is a psychological pattern in which a successful individual doubts their skills, talents, or accomplishments and has a persistent internalized fear of being exposed as a "fraud," despite supporting evidence to the contrary.

Put another way, it's when high-achieving people externalize their successes and internalize their failures. When high-achieving people don't feel at home in their achievements, it goes beyond the healthy nervousness of doing something new. Imposter syndrome is marked by a persistent sense of stress, anxiety, and feeling "I don't belong here."

Imposter syndrome does not discriminate. It impacts people of all gender identities and racial ethnicities. It impacts celebrities and the wealthy. It is extremely common, especially among high achievers.

In an interview, actor Tom Hanks described his imposter feelings. "No matter what we've done, there comes a point where you think, 'How did I get here? When are they going to discover that I am, in fact, a fraud, and take everything away from me?"

Oscar-winning actress Lupita Nyong'o said, "I go through [acute imposter syndrome] with every role. I think winning an Oscar may in fact have made it worse. Now I've achieved this, what am I going to do next?"

It's common for imposter syndrome to show up as feelings of anxiety around what you're great at and what should be enjoyable. Despite a previous track record of success, you may experience self-doubt, along with procrastination, overthinking, overworking, and an inability to accurately assess and communicate your skills in the workplace.

Imposter syndrome can sometimes be difficult to discern or understand. As dangerous as it is, it can produce positive outcomes on the surface, and some of the effects can actually be quite nice. You may be told you're "easy to work with," a "team player" with a humble spirit, or that you are really productive – more productive than most. Many professionals who deal with imposter syndrome deliver excellent professional work with few to no errors. The efforts of so-called imposters yield productivity for their teams and profitability for their companies.

Unfortunately, imposter syndrome doesn't come without costs to you.

Not feeling fully at home in our achievements costs us greatly. It costs us in the toll it takes on our mental health and well-being. It robs us of the ease we should experience when doing what we do best. It costs us physically in the toll the stress of perfectionism takes on our systems – think ulcers, headaches, depletion. Many people with imposter syndrome suffer physical exhaustion from overworking. It costs us financially in the lost earning potential from the opportunities we don't go after, or when we don't characterize ourselves and our achievements as powerfully as we could.

Working twice as hard often wins praise, accolades, and external success but this hypervigilance caused by imposter syndrome can increase overworking tendencies and increase the likelihood of burnout. That may look like expending more time, more effort, and more mental energy on tasks and decisions that should be easy. But this insidious cycle leads to feelings of exhaustion, increased mental distance, negativism, and cynicism.

The Paradox of Ease

One of the ways imposter syndrome showed up in my coaching work was with clients who were not "at home in their achievements" and were less willing to put themselves out there, go up for a promotion, or pitch themselves for new opportunities. On an even more basic level, when I'd help rewrite their bios or reframe their career narratives for LinkedIn, they'd often balk at a glowing description of their accomplishments.

It makes logical sense. Most high achievers are so close to their genius skill set that they can't clearly see what others see. Their natural gifts come easily, and they become easy to dismiss, diminish, and downplay. This is what I call "the paradox of ease."

But think about the cumulative toll this mindset can take on your career. If you're constantly mentally downplaying your achievements to yourself, it's hard to publicly position yourself for the promotions or pay your talents deserve. So you end up overworking to earn below your market value. And factor in those of us who are working simply to feel worthy, and it's the perfect setup to burn yourself out at work.

"Syndrome" Sounds Like a Personal Failing, but Systemic Issues Contribute to Imposter Feelings

But what causes imposter syndrome? Being or feeling different in some way can cause it, such as being a woman in a roomful of men, or a non-native English speaker in a roomful of native English speakers.

Bias and gaslighting in workplaces can exacerbate imposter syndrome, and unfortunately workplace gaslighting abounds. If you're given a set of benchmarks that you consistently exceed yet are told during your performance review that you're only meeting expectations, this can exacerbate imposter feelings.

Machine mindset creates fertile ground for imposter syndrome to flourish. Many professionals put machine-level productivity expectations on themselves. But we are not machines.

> According to the *Harvard Business Review* (February 2021), "The answer to overcoming imposter syndrome is not to fix individuals but to create an environment that fosters a variety of leadership styles in which diverse racial, ethnic, and gender identities are seen as just as professional as the current model."

Most high achievers will experience imposter syndrome at some point in their careers. It's a super common phenomenon, and it's not your fault. But understand that overcoming a bout of imposter syndrome doesn't make you immune to it; it will be a potential reality as long as you're leveling up. It will be triggered by every new level you achieve in your career. When there are new and perceived higher expectations, imposter syndrome is usually not far behind. This is why it keeps coming back whenever you experience a new project, a new job or promotion, or a new stage on which to share your gifts.

Ideas to Consider

Activating a project requires a different type of energy than maintaining a project. You won't always have to work as hard to maintain something as you had to work to get it off the ground. If you are a high achiever who has grown accustomed to striving and overworking on autopilot, that may feel unfamiliar to you. But at some point after you've put in the work, understand that the work will become easier. The trick here is to remember you've earned the ease. You don't have to tear down what you've built to make it hard again. Instead, now you can reinvest your time, energy, and effort into something else that means a lot to you. Now you can channel the energy you previously used to get this dream off the ground and put it into something else.

Or you can rest.

Key Insights

- "Work twice as hard" is widely circulated counsel that has been passed down through generations and accepted as good advice. Coupled with machine mindset, this advice has set us up to overwork on autopilot.

- For overachievers, the idea that a strong work ethic is the most important tool you have to reach one's goals has been passed down as gospel. This is a social norm that is not true.

- The **paradox of ease** is the idea that our true gifts and best contributions are the things that come easiest to us, but because we're so close to our genius skill sets we downplay, diminish, and devalue our skills to ourselves and to the world.

- The definition of burnout from the World Health Organization (WHO) ignores personal life, but we are people and dynamic. There are different types of burnout. The causes I list are not exhaustive.

- Overworking on autopilot refers to the act of pushing through and ignoring human needs after a health event, crisis, death, trauma, or other serious personal happening.

3 | Back-Burnering What Matters

Another way machine mindset keeps us misaligned is via the practice of "back-burnering" what matters. This refers to the process of routinely denying yourself what feeds you as a person – your physical and emotional needs such as hobbies, passions, and relationships – in favor of working or meeting other people's needs. The inverse, front-burnering, is the idea of focusing more on what drives and energizes you.

Back-burnering what matters is characterized by six key beliefs:

1. I don't have time for the activities that energize me and the passions that call me.
2. I don't have time for the relationships that energize me.
3. It's okay if my work is not fulfilling if it pays the bills.
4. I can't afford to be my authentic self.
5. I don't know who I am, what I want, or what drives me and I can't afford to stop and reflect.
6. I don't have time to take care of myself – I have to work, produce, or care for others.

Machine mindset, which is closely linked to hustle culture, insidiously encourages us to deny ourselves the very things that bring us energy and joy: our hobbies, relationships, nature, purposeful work, authenticity, and our individuality.

Joy is generative, yet we deny ourselves access to our energy-generating joy.

I Don't Have Time for the Activities That Energize Me and the Passions That Call Me

I had a particularly burnout-prone season at the end of 2023. My husband had knee surgery that sidelined him for a few months instead of an expected few weeks. Unable to drive, walk without crutches, or even stand up for more than a few minutes, all of the physical work of the family – the chauffeuring to All-State Band tryouts, daycare drop-offs and pickups, running up and down the three flights of stairs in our house – fell on me.

Then my two-year-old came down with RSV (respiratory syncytial virus) and her fever spiked to 102. While she was sick, I would get up in the middle of the night to check her temperature, force a syringe of Motrin between her lips, and pray the fever would come down. In the morning I would administer breathing treatments to give her tiny lungs some relief. She was at home and out of daycare for nearly 10 days while I fell further behind on my work projects.

Eventually, prayerfully, she got better.

But just as she did, my cat of 11 years passed away suddenly. It was a Sunday afternoon and I was driving 40 minutes to my 11th grader's school so he could attend his school play. The cat and he were roommates. On the drive over, he told me, "I think CJ is dying." By Wednesday he was gone.

The day the veterinarian had come and taken his still warm body away in a basket, I couldn't bear to pull back the thin purple blanket and look at him one last time. I'd petted and talked to him and cried with him a few hours earlier while he was still alive and mewing vigorously. But I just couldn't bear to see him lifeless. So I pet his body through the blanket before the vet took him away.

The next day I pushed my daughter's stroller up the street to her neighborhood daycare. She was finally recovering from her lung infection and we were back to our regular routine and it all seemed . . . cruel.

It was a beautiful morning, the kind that surprises you a little bit and makes you smile when you step out into the sunshine for the first time. The autumn leaves were glistening in the sunlight and there was a slight breeze. It had rained the night before and the air was clean and crisp.

As I walked up the street, everyone around me seemed so normal – so on their routine – it felt unfair that I had to harbor the weight of this heavy season, burnout, and now grief as if it was normal.

I walked my daughter up the front steps and into the building. I must have looked awful because her teacher immediately asked me what was wrong. As soon as I uttered the words "My cat died," I felt like I was about to cry, and I collapsed into her arms and let her hold me for a few moments while I sobbed.

I dodged my daughter's line of sight before apologizing to her teacher and turning to head back down the steps.

For the next few days I'd have periodic crying spells that would come on quickly without much warning. I had to tiptoe around the subject of pets to avoid being reduced to a snotty mess. I cried so much my nose became congested and I couldn't smell or taste anything, not even the morning coffee I looked forward to so much.

At one point I wondered how long I'd have to fall apart in grief – weeks? days? – before no one cared enough to give me grace.

But the grief on top of burnout broke something open in me. Desperate for a distraction, I began to write.

I needed something to pour myself into. I needed a productive distraction from my grief. So I started scheduling interviews for my business column and book. When I first landed the column, I'd made a list of interesting people I wanted to chat with for it, almost in a doodling way. Like, how fun it would be to talk to this person, or I bet they'd have a thing or two to say about burnout, but I hadn't reached out before to ask.

Some of the people on my list were connections, people I knew or could get to. Others were strangers whose work I admired. A few were old colleagues I hadn't talked to in years. Regardless, I began reaching out.

"Just schedule the interviews," I told myself. "The writing will work itself out. But at least get some raw material to work with."

I began to put one foot in front of the other – scheduling interviews and having conversations and talking about this subject that I'm simultaneously researching while living my life.

I was invested in hearing everyone's story about burnout while I struggled with feelings of my own. I wanted to feel less alone and I wanted to see if anyone had figured out a way to cope, selfishly so I could employ their tips.

But more than that, I was determined to enjoy this huge accomplishment of landing a column and subsequently a book deal. I wanted so much to enjoy the process of writing because I'd been dreaming of doing so more publicly for years.

I was determined not to let writing become just another line item on my to-do list, another thing to make me feel bad about not accomplishing before the day was done. I had been waiting to be this person my whole life, after all.

And sure enough, a funny thing began to happen – the more hours each week I spent doing the thing I'd told myself for years I couldn't afford to spend time doing, the better I felt. At points it felt almost like I was sneaking to have these meaningful conversations, make connections, and write up these summaries.

Weirdly too, since I felt better and had more energy, I also had more mental space for the rest of my work. I started catching up where I'd fallen behind.

I couldn't believe it. Could the solution be that simple? To give myself permission to do the thing I didn't think was practical or lucrative only to realize it creates practical and lucrative opportunities and energy in other ways?

I Don't Have Time for the Relationships That Energize Me

This is a particularly pervasive thought that plagues high achievers. With work as the top priority, personal relationships tend to take a backseat. We've all seen the tired trope of the hard-working businessperson who does not know their family, and upon retirement find themselves living among strangers. This is a recurring theme in movies, but real life is not far behind. Many of the clients I work with who are climbing ladders – either corporate or entrepreneurial – have had to sacrifice their most important relationships as a result of overworking. At different points they've neglected seeing their children as much as they want, they've put off time with aging parents, and they've all but discarded the close friendships that once brought them the most joy.

Not long ago I coached a high-ranking executive who'd been recently promoted. She was settling into the demands of her new role and found herself struggling to keep her head above water, never feeling like she completed every item on her to-do list. She was drinking from a fire hose, as the saying goes, and always felt behind. But where she was most behind was in her personal life. She had completely neglected her friendships, and with her parents several states away and the demands of work being what they were, she told herself she didn't have time to visit them. Through the course of our work together, I helped her to see that her workload would likely never lighten due to the realities of the position. Instead, she'd have to carve out space and make decisions about which key relationships she wanted to invest more time in. We began the process of front-loading her calendar for the year, which included trips to visit her mother every other month. Seven months later, when her mother became ill and passed away, she was grateful for the intentional time she'd made to visit more regularly in the previous months. She was grateful to have interrogated and interrupted the message that she didn't have time for one of her most important personal relationships.

It's Okay If My Work Is Not Fulfilling If It Pays the Bills

For years, when telling my story, it went something like this. I started communications and marketing consulting after I had my first baby and was laid off from my newspaper reporting job. After that layoff, I drilled down into my strengths, played up my marketable skills, made a list of people who might take my call, and started dialing, looking for work.

Within three months I tripled my monthly income and was still working from home. Plus, since I was working remotely, I had the flexibility to spend more time with my new baby. (This was 2008, and back then that was pretty major – much more of a flex than it would be considered today.)

For years, I thought that was my business's origin story. But that season of burnout 15 years later made me realize it was *really* my dream deferral story. Sure, I'd built a business during the Great Recession and found a way to help support my family. That work had put me on the map and given me a sense of professional achievement in that wasteland of my late 20s and early 30s when I was trying desperately to figure out my career footing.

But it had also taken me off track for what I had always dreamed of doing. By allowing myself to pursue only the practical and profitable applications of my talents, I'd stopped giving myself permission to make room to write more creatively. And by not making room for what energized me, I was robbing myself of the much-needed energy I could have leveraged to climb out of burnout.

By the time I found myself in that space of grieving our pet, taking care of my husband after surgery, and tending to a very sick toddler, I had been struggling for months to get a handle on my life and get to a place where I didn't always feel like I was just barely scraping by energetically as a mom and in my career. And the only thing that provided relief and a sense of psychic rest was taking my creative dream off pause, and putting pen to paper.

Exhaustion and burnout are definitely caused by what we do. When we do too much, we can get overwhelmed and run down physically and mentally. But exhaustion and burnout are also fed by what we *don't* do. They're fed by what we don't give ourselves permission to do.

Deferred dreams eat away at you.

It seems counterintuitive to say, "Just do more and that will make you feel less tired." But for me, doing more of the right thing – the soul-affirming and life-giving thing I've wanted to do since I was a kid – seemed to do just that.

I Can't Be My Authentic Self

Another way we back-burner ourselves is through the idea that we can't be our authentic selves. Hiding who you are with others or code-switching – the act of changing one's language choices, mannerisms, tone of voice, or physical presentation to come across as more pleasing and acceptable – in professional settings is exhausting. For the neurodivergent this may show up as "masking." Even introverts are known to put on an extroverted show to come across as more palatable in the workplace. And over time, that spent energy can contribute to burnout.

Dr. Reba Peoples is a board-certified psychiatrist and emotional wellness expert. She says the remote work so many people experienced during the pandemic was magical for underrepresented groups, who don't always feel comfortable showing up as their authentic selves at work.

"It removed the additional burden that we carry of emotional labor – that work of listening and validating and holding space for other people's emotional experiences," Peoples explained. She also said that people who code-switch have to choose their words or tone of voice carefully so they don't get labeled stand-offish, difficult, or angry. "That's exhausting, and that's really done at your own expense, and it really impacts your own emotional well-being," she said.

Inauthenticity directly impacts burnout because the work never ends. According to Peoples, "I think a lot of us never really had room to just exhale. You're doing all this emotional labor at work, and then you come home and you have to manage your household. So there's never any time when you're just allowed to be." Peoples believes that the opening the pandemic created allowed more people room for introspection; they had the chance to examine what it means to be human, and what it means to have a life that has value, meaning, and purpose and not value that's tied to their capacity to produce labor.

The great exhalation Peoples describes backed up against the economic trend that is now widely known as the Great Resignation. After exhaling at the top of 2021, many workers chose to voluntarily resign from their jobs in order to rest or go in search of roles that offered more work-life balance, flexibility, and better working conditions or better pay.

I Don't Know Who I Am, What I Want, or What Drives Me and I Can't Afford to Stop and Reflect

In 2017, Amber Cabral was downsized from her corporate job. She was interviewing for new roles and crashing with her godparents while she figured out her life in the interim. Like many jobseekers, she was going through the motions, applying for every job she thought she could land so she could quickly get her life back on track.

When her godfather asked her a simple question, she realized she was going about her job search the wrong way. He brought it to her attention that she had all of her major needs met for food and shelter. She had ample savings to pay what few living expenses came her way. So she didn't have to settle for just any job.

"What do you want?" he asked her.

In that moment, she realized she wasn't sure. And her lack of clarity was driving a faulty decision-making process.

"As he was asking me what I wanted, what I realized was I was wanting what I have been told to want, which is a job that pays well, somewhere I can thrive," Cabral reflected. "But that somewhere you can thrive piece is driven by a lot of little things. What kind of relationships do I have? Am I healthy in my body? Do I live in a neighborhood I enjoy? What kind of food do I have access to eat? That is a part of thriving as well."

Cabral says she began to consider her desires beyond a job and a paycheck. First she thought about what she didn't want. "I had seen what it felt like to work at a job that I didn't necessarily want to be at. I had known what it was like to live in a city I did not want to live in. I had known what it was like to be in environments that are fairly influential, but did not feel like they spoke to what I wanted. I knew what I did not want, so I used that to guide myself to the question of what do you want?"

At the same time, she was going through a three-month professional development training focused on personal branding, where each week she was having to think through what her brand was and how she wanted it to be communicated outside of just the work she did for an organization. So the class, coupled with her godfather's question, helped her see herself. She realized she felt differently when she was on a call doing a job interview than when she was talking about the work she wanted to be able to move forward with her personal brand.

Instead of focusing just on what she wanted to earn, Cabral says she began thinking deeply about how she wanted her life to feel, and let that information be her guide. She admits that sometimes it's easier for people to consider how they *don't* want life to feel when they have pointed examples of what doesn't feel great. But ultimately, knowing how we don't want to feel can lead us to how we do want to feel.

This deep self-inquiry was not only a personal wake-up call for Cabral, but it was also a strategy that allowed her to eliminate future work.

The clarity she cultivated by asking herself hard questions continues to pay dividends. She says she's been able to recover from episodes of burnout by regularly checking in with herself. "I still go back to it," she said. "I ask myself all the time, how do you want your life to feel?"

I Don't Have Time to Care for Myself – I Have to Work, or Care for Others

Putting other people above yourself, denying your needs to help another person, or deprioritizing your needs for the sake of someone else doesn't make your needs go away.

Even if you have a good reason for not taking time to meet your own needs – for example, your children need you, your sick parents need you, or your boss needs you to work extra hours – that good reason does not let you off the hook.

Your needs will call you. Your calling will call you, and regardless of what's going on with you personally or professionally, your calling is going to keep dialing until you answer.

What does that look like when you deny your needs and don't answer? What happens when you ignore what you can clearly hear? Irritation, anger, resentment, inability to focus, depression, sadness, anxiety, and overwhelm are all clues that you are backburnering yourself and what matters in some way.

Key Insights

- Overworking, machine mindset, and burnout or hustle culture insidiously encourage us to deny ourselves the very things that give us energy: joy, hobbies, relationships, nature, purposeful work, authenticity, and our individuality.

- **Joy is generative**, yet we deny ourselves access to our energy-generating joy. Start front-burnering what matters:
  - Make time for activities that energize you and carve out the space to pursue the passions that call you. Find ways to fit them into your schedule, even if it's just a little bit at a time.
  - Prioritize relationships that bring you energy and joy. Spend time with people who lift you up to help you keep burnout at bay.
  - Where you can, try to embrace and express more of your authentic self. Where it is safe to do so, have the courage to show up as you really are, both at work and in your personal life.
  - Take the time to reflect on who you are, what you want, and what drives you. What do you want? How do you want your life to feel?
  - Prioritize time for self-care, balancing work with personal well-being. Taking care of yourself is just as important as getting your work done – if not more so.

4 | Repeatedly Skipping Winter

Quiana Smith experienced her greatest level of burnout during the pandemic. In fact, she says she's still coming out of it.

Two things led to her burnout. First, she started a new role at a global consulting firm. Second, she believed she had to quickly prove herself and prove her value, which led to overworking. She says she'd been conditioned to overextend and overcommit herself throughout her career. But all that overextending caught up with her during the pandemic.

Smith was frustrated because she was tired of feeling she had to show up that way to be valued. "When I took the role I really was a one-woman band and the responsibilities for that role honestly required at minimum three people. So I'm doing the work of three people, which is, you know, enough within itself, but this is also during COVID and I'm also in the government practice. So the government is trying to figure out what the heck is going on and how do we respond to get our citizens what we need. So that's on all levels of government, all these tasks and requests are coming to us.

"And so it's responding. It's layered because I just started this job. So I want to prove my value on the job in general. And then there's the layer of, oh, my God, we are in a global crisis. And the industry that I support is really at the center of solving it. So now I'm at the center of solving it. So there's another layer of pushing myself beyond the point that I typically would to get that done. And so that caused me to be in every single meeting, almost every meeting that we had around the services and solutions that we provide."

Smith says she would get up in the morning around 8 a.m. and not leave her desk until 9 p.m. She wouldn't stop to eat, drink water, or exercise. "Before this, I'm someone who's in the gym four times a week, lifting weights. So I've shocked my body completely because it's malnourished. There's no exercise. I became anemic. And just completely exhausted."

She says she believes this unsustainable pace led to a promotion within two years – record time for the industry. But it came at such a high cost that it was anti-climactic.

"I was grateful for it, but it didn't feel like something that I should be celebrating because of what I had to do, what I chose to endure, and what I put my body through to get it," she said. "I have vowed that I will never do that again. And I have not."

Repeatedly Skipping Winter

One of the ways machine mindset keeps us misaligned is via the practice of repeatedly skipping winter. This refers to the act of not taking periodic breaks and getting rest after regular periods of working. Whereas overworking on autopilot refers to ignoring one's human needs in the face of grief or personal crisis, repeatedly skipping winter refers to the act of opting out of the standard rest one needs from periods of regular work – crisis or not.

Repeatedly skipping winter is characterized by four key beliefs:

1. I always have to be "on" even when I don't feel my best. I can't afford to take my foot off the gas or else I'll be passed over. I can't afford to disappear or else I'll be forgotten.

2. Access to technology means I have to show that I am being productive.
3. Blooming – aka visible work – matters more than invisible work that is happening underground. I can't afford to be invisible.
4. I don't have to make time to reflect, plan, and strategize for my future.

Winter is not a sexy season, but it is essential. The work of winter is quiet and private, but sets up the other seasons.

Blooming is rewarded by our jobs, fans and followers, society, and families. Achievement creates a visible indication of progress and invites external validation.

I Always Have to Be on Even When I Don't Feel My Best

In 2021, I hit a wall.

At the end of 2020, I delivered a baby by complicated cesarean section. On the operating room table, my doctor discovered that extensive scar tissue had formed since my last pregnancy and several of my organ walls had fused together. What started out as a routine procedure quickly turned into a risky and potentially dangerous operation. The procedure took several hours, and afterwards my doctor said my uterus was pretty beat up and she strongly advised against more children.

I let that news soak in back in my recovery room . . . with my laptop open. I was one of those people you hear about sending work emails from her hospital bed because I couldn't stand the thought of not "working to earn my keep." So of course once I was back home with my newborn baby, I chose to forgo maternity leave and continued working.

Perhaps most interestingly, I am a business owner and made the *decision* to put my postpartum pain aside to attend to clients instead of taking leave.

In my defense, I was gearing up for one of my busiest seasons in business. I was supporting my stable of executive clients, a group cohort of my personal branding academy, as well as two other group cohorts of employees at two client corporations. I was doing all of this while attempting to bond with my newborn daughter.

Light work for me, normally. But the superhuman feat of bringing a life into the world and acting as if that was just like making a cup of coffee was nonsensical.

I experienced a burnout unlike anything I've ever had before. In retrospect this is fascinating because having trained myself over a lifetime to overwork, there was always a bit more exertion available to squeeze out of myself at any given time.

It wasn't until that year that I finally reached the limit and crashed into my own wall of limitation.

Ironically, though, I had some of the most profound coaching moments and insights of my career during that time. I developed new frameworks for messaging and storytelling and deepened my own understanding of the *Purposescaping* executive coaching philosophy I'd started developing a few years prior.

When all of my group work expired in June, I followed it up with a much-needed (albeit probably too short) sabbatical. I returned in the fall and made plans to start another group but couldn't bring myself to. My usual window to launch another group cohort came and went. I kept telling myself next month, but next month would always feel too early.

My practice of repeatedly skipping winter had finally caught up with me.

Access to Technology Means I Have to Show That I'm Being Productive

When personal computers and work emails made communication about work easy, constant communication quickly rose as the expectation. When smartphones made responding effortless, responsiveness increased as a value by which to judge performance. And when social media gave the layperson a 24-hour stage on which to be seen, the urge to overwork in order to remain visible grew stronger, and the overworking muscle memory became even more deeply entrenched.

Whereas terms like "24-hour news cycle" are now the norm, information wasn't always so readily available and accessible until the last 20 or so years. But if information and communication are available 24 hours a day now and you're looking for a way to stand out, rise up, and get ahead, being "always on" is one way to do it.

I remember when Twitter drove traffic to my business. I pre-wrote tweets and scheduled them through an RSS feed to keep a constant stream of content coming even while I slept. (RSS, which stands for Really Simple Syndication, is an online file containing information about all the content a site has published.) In retrospect, this was pure insanity! Yet I wanted to give the perception of being on at all times, and to my regret I taught others to do the same. It felt necessary in those early career years. Hungry to make a name for myself, I unwittingly set myself to fall into the trap of overworking on autopilot by creating an expectation no one even asked me for.

I was terrified to take my foot off the gas of my career. Out of sight, out of mind scared me; I felt I could not afford to be forgotten.

I Can't Afford to Be Invisible

Blooming – visible work – can feel like it matters more than the invisible work that happens behind the scenes, and we want to avoid feeling invisible.

For almost two years after moving to a new home during a pandemic, my house sat half-empty as I waited for furniture to arrive. I felt very self-conscious in my space, knowing that projecting an image of success is important if you want people to "follow" you.

Then I had my daughter and as my weight fluctuated, I felt self-conscious about showing my pudgy face and my double chin. The social media posts crawled to a stop.

When my son noticed I hadn't posted in a few days, he asked me what was up. I felt horrible about messing up my posting streak. But I didn't have it in me to post. Something had to give.

So when it came time to package my daily experience into a neatly cropped photo to proclaim to the world "I'm okay! I'm doing great, actually. Perfect. Better than ever," I didn't have the functioning brain cells let alone the 20 minutes needed to stage, take, and filter said photo and write the accompanying thought-provoking, always introspective caption. I wanted to post, to share, to send a dispatch from my day-to-day, but I just didn't have it in me to do it.

What was I going to post about anyway? How I'd dropped off my crying daughter for her first day at daycare but was too exhausted to turn back or feel anything remotely close to guilt for leaving her there? How the weight I'd lost from breastfeeding was already quickly making its way back onto my stomach and thighs? How I was unglamorously and unsuccessfully troubleshooting the moldy smell coming from the basement?

I felt like a failure. A fraud. Someone who had encouraged everyone else to "put themselves out there" like I did on the backs of social media, as I snuck away from the spotlight and out the back door.

Then, in her Emmy acceptance speech, writer and actress Michaela Coel said, "Visibility these days seems to somehow equate to success. Don't be afraid to disappear. From it. From us. For a while. And see what comes to you in the silence."

Those words hit me so hard. Her speech felt like a message from the heavens. I saw that quote reposted hundreds of times in the 48 hours after the speech, as people echoed Coel's sentiment about stepping back from the limelight of social media and turning inward to protect their peace.

I found myself just wanting time alone – in person, online, every-where. I just wanted to be left alone and not be needed for once. I'd been going and going and thinking and strategizing nonstop for everyone else – masterminding private school applications and spring break plans and masked pandemic playdates while simultaneously an-swering each and every client whim.

But after the sense of failure dissolved, I felt an odd something akin to freedom. Truth be told, I was tired of the constant hunt for relevance, the thirst that seemed both desperate and demeaning. After I thought about it for a while, it seemed so silly to attempt to game the system to attract more followers I wasn't really leading anywhere.

Since downshifting my social presence in 2022, I have yet to fully ramp back up. I do post, but I don't have a regimented schedule to keep at the moment, though that could always change.

And yet . . . it's hard to ignore the nagging feeling that we don't always feel like we can take our collective foot off the gas. At least for me and my line of work, social media has been the gas pedal for a long time. There is so much angst in making the most of your opportunities to strike while the iron is hot. Crossing the threshold of 40, we feel ourselves to be in our prime yet are wise enough to know that some of our best years are behind us. So with the wisdom of experience we're working to maximize all the things – our degrees of privilege, our professional networks, our high-income city, relative youth, a good hair day, 15 minutes of caffeine-fueled effervescence – and strike before those proverbial irons cool.

My mom used to say, "You need to make hay while the sun is shining," which basically equates to get it while the getting is good, as if this could all be snatched away, or I'll look up at 50 and wish I'd maximized my earning potential – the potential to build networks, and promote myself online while I could. Because life is not always as forgiving, you feel like you can't take your foot off the gas, because if you do you'll be forgotten and slide into irrelevance.

I think about how I used to require myself – totally self-imposed – to impart some bit of wisdom or key insight daily online, whether or not I had it to give. But these days, I acknowledge that I just don't have it.

I Can't Afford to Take My Foot off the Gas or Else I'll Be Passed Over

One of my executive clients – an executive director of a nonprofit organization – didn't take a vacation for years. Instead, she took work home on the weekends. She took on the workload of four to five people, leveraging her background to develop strategies, conduct research, issue reports, plan events, and raise funds. While she had ample paid time off (PTO) on paper, as the organization's leader with visibility to each program need, challenge, and shortfall, she felt obliged to fill the gaps to ensure the organization maintained its high-quality work.

She regularly took work home and worked well into the evenings each day. This went on for years.

While she personally wasn't at risk for being passed over within her organization, her profile made her successes and failures more visible within the wider industry. Her job was secure and there was technically no promotion to be gained for overworking, yet she never took her foot off the gas. The phantom fear of failure chased her as she worked season after season without a break. It took a health crisis for her to finally stop and take some time off.

I Can't Afford to Disappear or Else I'll Be Forgotten

Stacey Ferguson set off a chain reaction in her personal life that started with changing her unhealthy relationship to work. Ferguson had been running Blogalicious – an online community of multicultural influencers that culminated in a signature conference each year – for nearly a decade, but in 2017 she began to feel a shift. She was creating content as an online influencer herself, managing a network of influencers of color, and hosting an annual conference under her brand. But she found in 2017 that her sponsor-supported business and network of online influencers were having a harder time garnering the same returns as they had in previous years.

"The budgets were getting smaller and there were more people competing for them, so it was getting harder to maintain the same level of revenue," she said. "The sponsors I'd been working with were demanding so much more and wanting to spend so much less."

But then she had a hysterectomy, and a complication during surgery landed her in the hospital for longer than expected.

"Right before the conference, we normally did pop-up events in different cities to generate excitement and sell tickets for the conference.

And we had four events planned and I couldn't go to any of them because I was in the hospital," she shared.

So she called in favors and had friends stand in for her. She made it to the conference, but afterwards she knew something had to change. "In my mind, I was going to take a break to rethink, 'What does influencer marketing look like in this new era – what is a business model? Does it make sense?'"

Amid contemplation, a friend reached out to tell Ferguson about a consulting opportunity she might be interested in. Exhausted and still healing, the offer came at just the right time. Initially, she planned to take a break from Blogalicious to recalibrate her life and get a handle on the business. But after going nine-to-five, she was surprised by how much the new pace suited her.

She ran communications and marketing for a series of startups before landing in her role as a VP at a mission-driven nonprofit organization clearing criminal records. "It's been almost six years," she said. "I never went back."

The new pace has improved her nervous system, but it wasn't easy. "I feel like it took me a long time to deprogram. Once you're on that hustle wheel it just becomes a way of life."

Before, she was always on, and that was a lot. Whether she was speaking at an event or meeting people afterward, she said she never knew from which direction the next opportunity would come, so she trained herself to stay on.

"Whether you're at a happy hour, in your mind this is a networking opportunity. As opposed to 'Oh I'm just here to hang out . . . ,' it's a different way of looking at life."

At night, after a busy workday in her business, she'd rush home to make dinner, do parent-teacher conferences, and take her kids to their sporting activities. Then after this second shift, she'd get back on her laptop, log on to conference calls, draft pitches, and create content for social media in bed until she fell asleep. And that became normal.

Before, she only got about four or five hours of sleep per night. But since sticking to a nine-to-five work schedule, she sleeps more.

Now she gets a blissful eight hours of sleep nightly and that's only one change she has experienced since going in-house.

She says she's happier, calmer, and has more time for friends. Before, her closest friends were never a part of her online world and didn't understand the realities of her influencer business. But now she has more time just to build those relationships and connect. "Now we just talk on the phone every day, multiple times per day," she said. "And it's cute – it's so cute."

For the last three years, she's done a vision board and included things outside of business, like her health, travel, and books she may read or even write. "Things that I've never made time to explore are now a part of my every day," she said. "So I just feel more well-rounded now."

Slowing down her work pace gave her back time to sleep, talk on the phone, and just be. It also set off the chain reaction by giving her room to face what was not working and make some key changes in her personal life.

While some of Ferguson's relationships began to thrive once she slowed down with work, the additional time and space to evaluate her connections meant that she could more easily see the ones that were no longer working for her. After 19 years, she and her husband ended their marriage.

"Once you opt out of the thing that keeps you busy, you're forced to sit with yourself a little more," she reflected. "Things that were maybe on the back burner before, now they're on the front burner just because you've made space."

Ferguson's story shows the pressure of feeling like you can't afford to disappear from the professional spotlight. She ran Blogalicious and managed a network of multicultural influencers for nearly a decade, driven both by her pride in what she'd built and a fear of being forgotten if she ever took a break. When she finally decided to step back and reevaluate her life, she ended up finding a much healthier work-life balance in a nine-to-five job.

The Mindset to Reject Rest

I'm not proud of this, but I used to judge people who didn't repeatedly skip winter – meaning they didn't sacrifice their well-being at the alter of overwork like I did. People who couldn't kick it into fifth gear or were limited or acknowledged their limitations for very valid reasons – like their commitment to child-rearing, parental care, personal boundaries, or the need to sleep – just weren't as committed, I thought.

But the last few years have changed me. I am sometimes still the queen of doing the most, but I realize now I am a mere mortal. I have had no choice.

If it hasn't been a school closure, it's been a COVID scare or losing someone to the pandemic. Maybe it's been the natural growth and maturity of aging, but I started giving myself and others way more grace than I used to. I've had to.

In the past I would have forced myself to map out an entire program around XYZ, or be unsatisfied with an article and feel like I needed to write a whole book! And if that resonates with you, it doesn't make you a wimp who isn't "excellent." It just makes you someone who is honoring healthy boundaries and the limitations that were always there, whether you knew they were or not. It makes you human.

This pandemic has changed my approach but also my values. It doesn't have to be so hard. It can be easy. And being easy doesn't make it any less valuable. It doesn't make me any less amazing or brilliant if I choose the path of least resistance and do what I can rather than doing the most.

Don't believe the lie that you have to make a grand entrance or have a grand offer to make. Do what you can.

And if what you can do is different from what you could do three years ago because understandably your capacity has changed, that's nothing to be ashamed of.

Nature as Our Guide

Humans have made it a habit of repeatedly skipping winter, which makes burnout inevitable. If we want to restore ourselves as living beings, we must look to the most elemental place for clues: nature and the natural world. To break unhealthy norms that we can and should be like machines, we must first accept the fundamental truth of our condition as just another living species, albeit a complex one. Like flowering plants, human beings have a season to sprout, a season to grow, a season to bloom, and a season to wilt. These seasons could map to four seasons of the year for simplicity's sake, and we'll look at this seasonal framework in more depth in Chapter 8.

Every Living Thing Needs Rest

We have adopted a machine mindset that ignores our biological needs and humanity and routinely ignored our need for rest. Until we stop ignoring our basic needs, we will forever vacillate and find our way back to exhaustion. Where overworking on autopilot refers to pushing through universal human events, repeatedly skipping winter refers to incessantly chasing the limelight of achievement and results with no regard for our human need for rest.

Why Skipping Winter Becomes Hard to Stop

When you're accustomed to treating yourself like a machine, it can be hard to rest. You may feel guilty. Rest takes ongoing practice. It requires you to continuously disrupt norms. You will backtrack and fall back on all patterns. But keep challenging and replacing them with your new ideas.

Key Insights

- Winter is not a sexy season, but it is essential.
- Blooming – aka external achieving – is rewarded by our jobs, fans and followers, society, and families. Achievement creates

a visible indication of progress and invites external validation, which can be addictive.

- The work of winter is quiet and private, but it sets up the other seasons.
- It's hard to bloom year-round.
- Skipping winter refers to not taking periodic rest after regular working. We do this because of machine mindset, social pressures, fear of becoming irrelevant, and guilt about not being productive.
- The relevance hunting caused by the need to keep up with social media leads to repeatedly skipping winter.
- Skipping winter happens not just because of social media but also email and all of the online communication channels that make it possible for work to follow us around.

5 | Burnout Breaking Point

As I started my research for this book, conversation after conversation pointed to a similar pattern that seemed to befall each person I interviewed. Before succumbing to burnout, each person described how machine mindset, overworking on autopilot, back-burnering what matters, and repeatedly skipping winter had kept them misaligned right up to the moment of a "burnout breaking point."

A burnout breaking point refers to a key life event that causes the record to skip on your overworking, forces you off autopilot, and makes you wake up to the unsustainability of your habits. For some, the burnout breaking point serves as the final awakening that pushes them forward to deprogram, recalibrate, and find a way forward without overworking. For others deeply entrenched in machine mindset, they are awakened only temporarily. They may consider a brief change of pace but ultimately will start the cycle all over again and go back to overworking on autopilot.

A burnout breaking point typically occurs after one of the following events:

- A health crisis
- The loss of a loved one
- A career aha moment, like a layoff, missed promotion, or stalling of opportunity

A Health Crisis

Imani Samuels was trained as a marketer and communicator and worked in-house for many years in advertising. In 2019, she experienced severe burnout where she worked an unsustainable number of hours on a big tech project. After a decade working for a large nonprofit, she switched to a new tech-focused team doing what she considered revolutionary work.

"It took a lot of change management and it required me to learn as I was going," Samuels told me. "And I think that because I was learning as I was building and we were up against really hard deadlines, I was just spending so much time trying to figure it out. And that required me to wake up early in the morning, to do as much work as possible, wake the girls up, haul them across town to school, go into the office, come home, work again, make a little bit of dinner, work again."

As she and her team worked to meet their deadline, this was her schedule for one particularly grueling season – 18 months of working weeknights, weekends, and early mornings she says felt like a lifetime. "It's a social mission, so there was goodness behind it. I felt good about the work that I was doing but it became debilitating. I developed anxiety," Samuels said.

That summer, before taking her children to stay with her parents for a few weeks, she noticed her eldest daughter had spots on her skin. It turns out the spots had developed over several months and Samuels hadn't noticed. She felt mortified as a mother and reached out to a dermatologist. The doctor told her that had it lingered any longer, her daughter could have developed skin cancer.

"That nugget of info completely changed the way I did life," Samuels declared.

The Loss of a Loved One

André Blackman founded Onboard Health – a search and advisory firm focused on placing diverse healthcare leaders – in 2017 to "power an equitable future of health." He saw an increase in need for his company's services during the pandemic, especially after the murder of George Floyd. But running a healthcare startup during the global healthcare crisis of COVID eventually took its toll. He began to burn out. Yet it was an increase in revenue, not a decrease, that began his spiral.

"I was building the company while also navigating a very aggressive uptick in needs for the services," he said. And from his perspective as a budding thought leader in the space, he felt a spotlight on him to have an opinion on the national healthcare conversation while simultaneously building a team and successfully leading a company. "There was a lot of pressure to perform well across the board."

As pressure was building at work, Blackman experienced a profound personal blow toward the end of 2021. His best friend contracted a breakthrough case of COVID and was hospitalized. From his hospital bed, the friend texted Blackman asking to talk. Blackman received the message while he was out of town at a conference and scrambled to respond.

"I wanted to get to a spot where I could hear clearly, and sit down and see him," Blackman said. He messaged his friend saying he'd call him back in 20 minutes but when he did, no one picked up. "Three minutes later, his wife called and she was in hysterics, saying how he was gone," Blackman recalled.

That sudden unexpected loss kicked off a period of grief that compounded Blackman's exhaustion. He found himself in "a deep burnout season."

As the pressure cooker of startup life pushed him into a corner, Blackman says it reminded him of his former industry – digital media. He'd come of age career-wise when social media exploded the field of communications, and suddenly PR practitioners were expected to churn out content and always be on. He began to experience anxiety symptoms much like those he'd experienced earlier in his career. He knew his pace was unsustainable, yet he soldiered on.

Then the unthinkable happened. Another close friend of Blackman's died unexpectedly, this time from complications of a rare blood clot that developed after a long flight. At that point, he couldn't push through anymore. He'd reached his burnout breaking point.

Like André Blackman, Amber Cabral was running her own boutique consulting firm when demand for her services grew so much that she had to expand her team from 5 to 10 people. The growth also meant she was often working 12- to 14-hour days and often at odd hours to accommodate her global clients in different time zones.

Cabral was already on the brink of burnout, but when her godmother had a heart attack and died suddenly in the summer of 2021, she decided finally to take some time. After the funeral, she booked a flight to Anguilla and took a week off to grieve and gather herself. Days into her vacation she realized she'd missed the deadline to submit a proposal to a major new client.

"I don't drop balls. That doesn't happen to me," Cabral said. "I don't miss opportunities. I don't do that. But I was just so exhausted that when I got to Anguilla, I let everything go."

After quickly trying to pull something together on vacation, she decided to come clean. "I started trying to type the proposal. I started working on it and my body was like, no – we're on vacation." She remembered her recently declared company values. "Health, rest, and well-being," she said. "That's the thing we should be focusing on."

She emailed the client, explaining her situation and that she couldn't make the deadline. Then she got back to her vacation.

"I needed the rest," Cabral said. "I am grieving."

A Career Aha Moment

Aundrea Cline-Thomas spent two decades working in local news. She'd won Emmy Awards, interviewed celebrities, and worked in a dozen small markets before landing the holy grail of local news – a role at a news desk in New York City.

She describes herself as a "very high-achieving, very leaned-on person in the newsroom." But after almost four years in New York, she needed more. "I was doing multiple jobs, and that wasn't reflected in a lot of different ways, compensation and in terms of my title," she said.

So she did the things the career books say to do. She had conversations about other opportunities within the company. Because her employer didn't want to lose her, they offered her another opportunity. But the offer just did not align with who she wanted to be at that point in her career.

"I had so much more potential than the opportunities would allow me to tap into. I had so much more desire and passion than the opportunities would allow me to exercise," Cline-Thomas told me. "And I'm a high achiever. I'm ambitious." Even with a new offer on the table, Cline-Thomas had reached her burnout breaking point. So she decided to leave.

It was complicated to be highly ambitious, innovative, and forward thinking in a space that didn't have an outlet for her. And since she was under contact, she couldn't moonlight or take on other work that would offer more fulfillment.

"It creates such a friction and a frustration," she said. "And so the only way is to jump off the proverbial cliff and just try something new. I knew I didn't want to just take another news job. I had done that. That was my fifth move."

She knew that even at another news station, the issues would follow her there. "There's parts of it that are inherently just going to be the same," she said. "And that's not what I wanted in my life. I wanted something different."

Key Insights

- You know something is unsustainable when it breaks you. But that breaking could be your signal to rest.
- Our commitment to machine mindset means that only when we are abruptly reminded of our humanity – usually through a crisis of some sort – will there be an opening for change.
- Pandemics and wars clarify values for society. The death of loved ones, health crises, and unexpected caretaking can serve to clarify values for individuals.
- There must be an event that makes the record skip and disrupts overworking on autopilot. Machine mindset is too strong and too deeply entrenched to interrupt on your own. It often takes a breaking point to bring you back to humanity.

6

Deprogramming, Recalibrating, and Front-Burnering

After overworking on autopilot, back-burnering what matters, and repeatedly skipping winter before eventually reaching a breaking point severe enough, many are inspired to finally start correcting the misalignments that have led to burnout. They do this by deprogramming, recalibrating, and front-burnering what matters. These terms all refer to the act of waking up to the reality that machine mindset is driving your warped sense of ambition. The deprogramming process is the courageous act of finally putting a stop to the overwork and self-betrayal that has fed burnout up to the breaking point moment.

But when you are accustomed to treating yourself like a machine, changing your approach is hard. Choosing an alternative to over-working – like resting – is not necessarily easy. Even when you decide to change your habits and reject old programming and do more things that feed your happiness, many find that they have to build in extra time to ease into the new healthier habits. It is not something you decide to do in one fed-up moment and quit cold turkey.

Just as you built up the habit of overworking, your recalibration requires some muscle memory as well. This is not a simple mindset shift; it is a whole system of mindset and spiritual adjustments – a new long-term practice of divesting from the overworking on autopilot that does not serve your humanity.

Deprogramming requires both practice and practices. Most people will be changing decades of programming, so the process will take time, and require patience. Expect to backslide.

Because your overworking tendencies typically benefit those around you, those people may not support your changes. Prepare to have to uphold your new boundaries and defend your new choices.

Deprogramming, recalibrating, and front-burning what matters to you are the beginnings of a lifelong process of reclaiming your humanity after years of approaching achievement and work with a machine mindset.

Decoupling Worth from Work

Myleik Teele overworked her way to a multimillion-dollar company. Curlbox, her monthly beauty subscription box and marketing company, served thousands of customers and shipped thousands of products each month at its height, which meant she was overworking for years. But in 2023 Teele had her own burnout breaking point, shuttered the company, and hasn't looked back.

"Working hard saved my life," Teele said. "So when I tell people that I'm not working as hard today, I would never take back what I did back then because I think it set me up to feel that now I can rest. So I don't regret that at all."

I first found Teele through her popular podcast where she doled out career advice in the tone of the big sister I never had but always wanted. I resonated deeply with Teele's episodes because, like me, she wasn't afraid of hard work. She was proof that even when the odds are stacked against you, which at times I felt they were for me, hard work could and would prevail.

But at some point she began to wonder to what end this was leading. "I think back to when I was starting out and it was like, all right, we can really hustle our way out of debt, out of the hood, we can do that. I think there were people who have done that and now people are just like, 'All right so what are we doing now? Because we're tired.'"

After repeatedly skipping winter for years, Teele found herself pregnant with her second child and more aware of what she wanted and didn't want. She'd started working to hire more employees so she could focus on parenting, but the more effort she put into hiring and people management, the more disenchanted she felt with the business.

"I knew I was going to have to take some steps back. I was just so far away from my zone of genius," she said. "I was so far away from what it is that I do. And my days were very difficult, and they were not what I wanted. I was trying to figure out, what do I do? I wanted to get out of my warehouse. I was trying to figure out how do I scale this down? Limit some of the people? How do I just make this work for me so that I can be a mom and be an entrepreneur?

"It was exhausting. I look back at that time in my life, like, what was I doing?" She realized she'd shipped over 100 months of back-to-back subscriptions. "I never got a break," she said.

When she finally reached what she thought was her breaking point, she was still negotiating with the business, trying to figure out ways to make it less hard for herself. She thought about hiring a creative director who could do the photo shoots for the subscription box, and an operations person who could run the day-to-day of the business. But that proved not to be the solution. "I knew that my lease was coming up. I was going to try to go to the end of this year. And then my mom died and I realized I was done. It was like, well, this is where our time concludes because I just wasn't feeling it."

After her mother passed away, Teele says she began questioning how she was spending her time and decided to make some changes. She shuttered the business and her once frenetic business pace crawled to a stop.

Reevaluating Ambition

An attorney by training, Stacey Ferguson of Blogalicious – whom you met in Chapter 4 – had always been ambitious, and the chance to flex her creative muscles drew her to online entrepreneurship. But since leaving that life behind in 2016, she admitted that she missed the action of her old influencer life. Being out of the online loop took some getting used to.

Some members of her community implored her to come back. As new online platforms began to heat up, she kept hearing about how she was missing out. But after a while, her appetite for the hustle faded.

"In the first three years [after leaving the business] I had that FOMO, like 'Oh gosh, what if I had continued doing blogging or influencer campaigns or Blogalicious,' and 'Look at all these people on Instagram.' And then one day, I just didn't care."

Away from the relentless pace of her former entrepreneurial schedule, Ferguson began to reevaluate why she was pushing herself so hard.

"Why am I doing this? What do I really want to do? Do I really want to be famous on social media?" she asked herself. "Or do I want to enjoy my work, log off at 5 p.m., and then go have drinks with my good friends whom I never see because I'm always working? I want to be present for my kids as they become young adults. Those questions became more important to me."

Understandably, this recalibration brought her professional identity into question. She had to figure out who she was outside of the popular online brand she had carved out. "If I no longer have Blogalicious, then who am I? Because it was my identity for so many years," she said.

Ultimately, she chose her newfound sense of freedom over the pull of more and more professional achievement. "When you're struggling with that decision, choose the decision that makes you feel free."

Recalibrate with Rest

One way Quiana Smith started getting rest was by detaching emo-tionally from what was going on at work. She started declining cal-endar invitations and questioning if her presence was truly needed at certain meetings. Before her promotion, she didn't have her own support team at work so she found people in other departments who could support her, and began to delegate.

"Before it was do the best work, it's all about the work. But that's not all that it takes to get promoted. You have to have relationships; you have to understand the politics of a firm," she said.

"Another thing I realized is that leaders can't be exhausted. They have to delegate, and the fact that I'm sitting here trying to do everything myself means I'm not even presenting myself as a leader."

Time and time again, once professionals are finally ready to start breaking the cycle of overwork and begin the reprogramming and recalibration process, they start fighting for rest in small, daily ways.

To help build intentional rest into her schedule, Smith got serious about her morning routine. She began starting her day with a short devotional or inspirational reading, followed by meditation to ground herself. She uses the Calm app or meditations by Deepak Choprah and Oprah to help her. The whole routine takes only about 20 minutes. And if she misses her morning 20 minutes, she feels it. "If I don't do it in the morning, I feel off, so I'll do it at lunch or at night before bed."

Reba Peoples, the psychiatrist you met in Chapter 3, found a replenishing morning routine important as well. She did what she calls "energy mapping" to understand which tasks were draining and which tasks were replenishing her energy. She used to start her days seeing patients but found that if she saw her clinical patients in the afternoon, she could have her mornings free for rest.

"When it is a scheduled appointment, that's something that has to be done, that's an obligation that I'm very good at following through with," Peoples said. "But I found that I was sort of not following through with my obligations to myself." She now starts her day with activities that make her feel rested – she practices qigong, reads, writes, and works on her independent passion projects.

Deprogramming, Recalibration, and Front-Burnering

After her godmother passed away, Amber Cabral, whom we met in Chapter 1, was overcome as her grief compounded the burnout she was already feeling. She was forced to make some changes to bring support and joy back into her life.

First, she asked herself how she wanted her life to feel. Next, she made a number of changes. To start, she hired a personal assistant to handle personal to-dos and the day-to-day management of her home. She was scheduled to move to a new apartment, and given her love of sunsets, only considered new homes with west-facing windows during her apartment search.

She was tired of putting things on the back burner that meant something to her. She began making time for her relationships. She traveled to Las Vegas to see singer Usher in concert – twice. She began having friends over and entertaining in her home again.

Cabral decided to invest in "things that fuel my resilience." When it comes to resting, relationships, and travel, she has a new attitude. "This is the life part," she said. "I'm not putting [life] on the back burner anymore."

Honoring Her Needs

On the Friday after Thanksgiving, Lenise Williams lounged on her couch reading while her son – a freshman at Louisiana State University – caught up on Netflix shows nearby. Though it was the day after a major holiday, she was haunted by a lingering sense of uneasiness.

"It felt weird," Williams said. "The whole time I was resting and not on the computer, I felt like I should be on the computer, like I should be doing something else."

Williams is the owner of Made, a leather goods store with an e-commerce shop. She sells her products almost exclusively online and Black Friday is typically one of her business's busiest days.

But this year, Williams just didn't have the juice. "Black Friday is not just about a sale that day; it's about preparing, checking the inventory, preparing flyers, preparing emails, and then having to ship all of that stuff out," she explained. "And when I thought about it, when I started organizing it, I felt like I just don't want to do this."

Her small team that works with artisans out of Marakesh was on the same page. Just two months earlier, a 6.8-magnitude earthquake had decimated the Moroccan city where the leather artisans who supply her leather products live and work.

"I think we all felt the same way this year, with that earthquake. It was just draining for us," Williams said. "Once we sat down and got ready to do it, we all just were like, 'We're tired.'"

So instead of prepping her sale and watching her site, Williams took a moment to catch her breath. Instead of logging on ready to work like she normally does, she used the long holiday weekend to enjoy family and spend time with her son, who was home from college.

"I miss him," Williams said of her son. "I want to hear about school, and I want to see how much he's matured. I don't want to tell him, 'Hey, I have to go because we have to ship packages.' I just wanted to be still and be present in the moment."

When she shared her intention not to run a Black Friday sale with her Instagram followers, some fellow business owners were supportive. But quite a few weren't. "They thought I was crazy," Williams said. "One person even told me, 'That's not a smart business move.'"

Remember, as you recalibrate, not everyone around you will support your changes – especially when those changes create more work or generate less money for them directly. Prepare yourself to defend your new choices.

Dr. Adia Gooden says skipping a big sale may be financially costly, but it is worth it in terms of impact on a business owner's mental health. "Much of the business advice out there leaves entrepreneurs feeling like they must constantly hustle to make more and more money. This often ignores the mental and emotional cost of constantly working and selling," Gooden explained.

Gooden often encourages women to accept that they're enough, and she believes that any business advice should be considered in the context of your own mental, emotional, and physical needs.

What did Lenise Williams need? Rest.

So she cooked, ate, and spent her first Thanksgiving weekend in years offline. Her son watched movies on Netflix while she indulged in a rare pleasure – reading fiction. She read two books cover to cover over the weekend.

More importantly, she and her son were both present for the time they spent together – something she wouldn't have been able to be had she been running a high-stakes e-commerce sale.

Finding New Methods

The process of writing this book has been a fantastic teacher. Not only has it made me confront my own habits of overworking – the kind of habits that lead to burnout – but it's also forced me to devise new strategies and new approaches to get the results I am accustomed to without wearing myself out.

At one point when I hit an impasse in the writing process, I felt a sense of overwhelm and frustration come on. The voice of the old me was punitive and encouraged me to push through, chain myself to my desk, and throw some more effort at it until the answer came.

But there was a gentle tugging, tugging at me to pick up the phone and call a friend to whine about my problem. I chose to give myself the luxury of support instead of staying stuck isolated in my overworking. I made the call.

By the time I hung up the phone an hour later, I had five new insights, one of which was the very solution that I needed for the problem that prompted me to pick up the phone in the first place.

That was a profound moment for me, and I have had many during the course of this particular writing journey.

We really can do things differently. There is another way. We can still get great results at work without overworking to the point of burnout.

We just have to listen to ourselves and tune into our needs. When we do, we can form new practices and build new habits that are restorative and kind.

Key Insights

- This is not a simple mindset shift, it is a system of mindset and spiritual shifts – a lifelong practice of divesting from the overworking on autopilot that does not serve your humanity.
- As you recalibrate away from overworking, you will backslide. You are changing decades of programming, and the process both takes time and never ends. Be patient with yourself.
- Deprogramming requires practice and practices.
- Society may not support your changes because your overworking tendencies tend to benefit those around you. Prepare yourself to defend your new choices.
- Deprogramming is the first step in reclaiming the humanity you gave up for machine mindset.

7
Origins of the Modern Burnout Epidemic

The late 1800s ushered in a number of critical shifts that would set the stage for the machine mindset that claimed the life of folk hero John Henry, the hard-working rail worker who dropped dead from exhaustion after winning a race against a steam drill. Those shifts also planted the seeds that would eventually grow into practices like over-working on autopilot that laid the early groundwork for the modern burnout epidemic in America.

First, the US Civil War (1861–1865) split the Northern and Southern states and claimed 620,000 lives. Slavery was legally abolished in 1865 and four million African Americans were legally freed. Many became paid laborers, although segregation laws, violence, and discrimination made it difficult for newly freed Blacks to gain their footing in society.

As slavery was abolished and the South began to rebuild after war, industrialization and urbanization were rapidly transforming northern cities. Manufacturing increased, railroads like John Henry's were built by Black and immigrant labor, and steel mills anchored northern cities and attracted people seeking work.

Immigrants fleeing religious persecution, famine, and political instability at home poured into the United States in search of opportunity. Bringing their religious practices, customs, music, and food, they played an important role in shaping American culture and provided a steady supply of labor for the budding industries of the rapidly industrializing country.

These big changes shaped the work, the future of work, and the work of three important thinkers, who offer clues both to how we got to the current burnout epidemic as well as potential solutions for restoration.

Frederick Winslow Taylor

By the late 1800s, Frederick Winslow Taylor was working as a chief engineer at the Midvale Steel Company in Philadelphia when he spied another opportunity to apply his training. As a laborer and machinist, Taylor had observed inefficiencies that made labor costs skyrocket at the plant. He quickly rose up the ranks at Midvale working as a machine shop laborer, then a time clerk, a machinist, machine shop foreman, and eventually chief engineer.

When he was promoted to foreman, he decided he wanted to improve the outcomes of his staff members so he studied the worker productivity of both his men and the machines they used to come up with suggestions to streamline their processes. He dove into this work and conducted a number of experiments, called time-and-motion studies, where he would meticulously observe the individual human movements required to perform each task and record the slightest variations that could improve or decrease productivity. Taylor was in search of what he would eventually term the "one right way" to perform a task well. Using his understanding of machines as a mechanical engineer, he observed that as new industries emerged, companies were struggling across the board to produce consistent, uniform, predictable outputs. This process began an entirely new field of study that became known as scientific management.

By 1893, Taylor began his own consulting practice in which he offered services to systemize shop management and lower manufacturing costs. In 1898, he took on Bethlehem Steel as a client. By 1911, he had worked with several large companies and found great success as a consultant sharing the best practices and case studies he'd uncovered while working as a consultant. He began traveling around to share his findings, the outcome of his experiments, and his papers.

By 1910, Taylor was in demand as a management consultant helping companies like Bethlehem Steel analyze their workflows, standardize processes, and train employees to efficiently produce and perform in a consistent way. He had also solidified his position as a pioneer in management theory. He's now known as the father of scientific management and his work is referenced and studied widely. He published *The Principles of Scientific Management* in 1911, sharing his best practices for worker productivity and manufacturing efficiency that are an enduring influence on workplaces more than 100 years later.

Henry Ford

As the country neared the turn of the century, another engineer was building his career in Michigan. Henry Ford was working at Edison Illumination Company in Detroit, gaining experience as an engineer and experimenting with engine designs for his first motorized vehicle on the side. By 1893, he'd successfully motorized an early version of the automobile – the quadricycle, which was essentially a motorized horseless carriage on bicycle wheels. In 1903, he founded Ford Motor Company and by 1910 had revolutionized yet another burgeoning industry of the industrial age – automotives.

Building on Frederick Taylor's work in productivity and efficiency, Ford innovated manufacturing techniques to include the moving assembly line, which went on to become widely adopted by other manufacturers and is still seen in today's factories. Ford's Model T automobile democratized private transportation, transforming how people moved about the country, while his production methods transformed industrial practices around the world.

George Washington Carver

While engineers and entrepreneurs like Frederick Taylor and Henry Ford focused on improving efficiency to cut costs and drive manufacturing productivity and profit in the wake of the Industrial Revolution, a Black scientist was working on a different type of productivity.

George Washington Carver had been born into slavery around 1864 in Diamond Grove, Missouri, just as the Civil War was coming to a close. As an infant, he was kidnapped by slave raiders along with his mother. He was recovered by the Carvers – the white couple that owned his family – but his mother was never seen again.

After slavery was abolished, Carver and his brother stayed and worked on the small farm of the white couple who had enslaved them before the war. From an early age, Carver displayed a passion for learning and an aptitude for botany and agriculture. Hungry for knowledge, he walked eight miles to attend his first school in nearby Neosho, Missouri. Though academically gifted, Carver found it challenging to get an education because most schools didn't accept Black students. When he attended schools designated for Black children, he quickly outgrew the curriculum and surpassed the other students.

Nevertheless, Carver persevered. He eventually attended Simpson College in Iowa before transferring to Iowa State, which was an unheard of feat for a Black person in post–Civil War America.

Carver earned a BS in agriculture in 1894, becoming the first African American to attend and graduate from Iowa State. When he earned a master of science in 1896, that degree gave him the added distinction of being the first African American to receive an MS in agriculture.

By 1896, George Washington Carver was living the dream. He was degreed and working in his field as an assistant botanist at the Iowa State College experiment station. It was there that he received a letter that would change his life.

Booker T. Washington, the esteemed president of the Tuskegee Institute – a training school for Black students in Alabama – had heard of Carver's accomplishments. Washington invited Carver to leave his post in Iowa to come teach, work, and run his own department at Tuskegee. But the school administrator couldn't offer much.

"I cannot offer you money, position, or fame," Washington's letter to Carver read. "The first two you have. The last from the position you now occupy you will no doubt achieve. These things I now ask you to give up. I offer you in their place: work – hard work, the task of bringing people from degradation, poverty, and waste to full manhood. Your department exists only on paper and your laboratory will have to be in your head."

Although he had to take a pay cut, Carver immediately accepted the position and headed south to Tuskegee. But upon arriving in Alabama, Carver was struck by what he saw. Throughout the South, where farmland stretched for acres at a time, the soil was utterly depleted. The poor tenant farmers, also known as sharecroppers, were barely surviving.

After years of one-crop agriculture, growing cotton – the demand for which had exploded due to advances in textile manufacturing – the soil was missing key nutrients. As a result, the poor Black farmers – many of them sharecroppers struggling to make ends meet – were having trouble getting their land to produce a good yield.

In short, the soil was facing its own severe burnout. Using his knowledge of agricultural science, Carver began teaching Southern farmers near Tuskegee how to restore their depleted soil through simple agricultural methods like crop rotation. He taught them that by rotating what they grew they could add nutrients back to the soil (a practice that would later become part of organic farming). He encouraged the farmers to plant soil-restoring crops like sweet potatoes, soybeans, and most famously peanuts – plants that both restored key nutrients to the soil and could be used to develop other products that could be consumed or sold. By rotating crops, farmers could restore the soil's ability to produce.

As we seek to understand and find solutions to our modern burnout pandemic, Carver's approach can give us clues to restoration. Around the same time that management theorists were tackling new workplace challenges sparked by the Industrial Revolution, Carver was finding solutions for agricultural burnout in the Southern farming states. Both Frederick Taylor, a mechanical engineer by training, and Henry Ford, an engineer turned entrepreneur and titan of manufacturing, focused on improving worker efficiency by developing methods that helped human workers mimic machines. This productivity drove down labor costs and drove up profits.

Carver, on the other hand, was focused on restoring productivity in other ways. With the goal of helping his people – descendants of slaves, poor tenant farmers – survive, Carver devised sustainable, restorative farming methods that in turn increased production.

Crop rotation solved burnout of the soil. Traveling throughout the South in his "Jesup Wagon" – a mobile classroom and laboratory wagon – Carver distributed short bulletins like "How to Build Up Worn Out Soils." These bulletins included simple instructions explaining agriculture in layman's terms. Recognizing the need to take lessons on agriculture to rural farmers where they were, Carver brought the Jesup Wagon into communities and conducted agriculture workshops and demonstrations as a part of his community outreach.

He successfully encouraged farmers to plant nitrogen-fixing crops of peanuts, soybeans, and sweet potatoes. Carver helped farmers restore an income-producing yield, diversify their production, and generate new sustainable sources of food and income.

Whereas Frederick Taylor transferred his training in mechanical engineering to people and mapped out ways for human beings to better perform like machines, Carver did the opposite. I like to think that because Carver was trained in the science of plants and his native source materials were living things, his methods offer transferable insights for the restoration of other living beings.

Years later, George Washington Carver and Henry Ford met in Michigan at a meeting of pioneers in the chemurgy movement (the science of creating industrial products from agricultural raw materials). Ford, who had also grown up on a farm, was looking for ways to integrate agricultural crops like soybeans into his automotive production process and create plant-based fuel, paints, and the like for use in vehicle production. Both at the top of their respective games in the late 1930s, the two went on to form a friendship and wrote letters back and forth for several years.

Ford reportedly picked Carver's brain about science and the two collaborated on several projects together. From time to time, Carver looked in on the crops at Ford's Georgia plantation and reportedly even helped him come up with a plant-derived rubber substitute during a World War II rubber shortage. At one point, Ford glowingly stated that Carver had taken Thomas Edison's place as "the world's greatest living scientist."

The Beginnings of Purposescaping

In 1961, seventh-grade students at Dunbar High School in the small town of Savannah, Tennessee, pooled their money from home economics class bake sales of cupcakes to send away for a black-and-white portrait of the late Professor George Washington Carver. Weeks later, the 18"×32" photograph of a stately Carter arrived, and Ruth Johnson Malone, who taught the seventh graders, hung it proudly in her classroom.

For the classroom of junior high school students, the framed image of Carver was a symbol – both of the work they'd done to earn the money to purchase it and the pride they felt for such an esteemed educator and member of their race.

In 1966, 12 years after *Brown v. Board of Education*'s landmark Supreme Court decision declared racial segregation in public schools unconstitutional, Dunbar, a school for Black students, graduated its last high school class. The brick building that sat at the intersection of Dunbar and Harlem Streets in Savannah was largely abandoned save for a few administrative offices. The back of the building also served as a bus depot for the county school system and stored other machinery. Later it was demolished to make room for the Hardin County Schools Transportation Department.

James Frank Sevier Sr. lived across the street from the abandoned school and had worked there while it was still operational. A former school bus driver and janitor for the school, he maintained an elaborate ring of keys that unlocked various rooms of the old school building for years. So when his daughter Mattie, who had been valedictorian of the school's final graduating class, requested the Carver portrait her classmates had pooled their money to purchase, he retrieved it for her.

She took the portrait with her when she moved to Nashville to continue her studies, and, once married and settled, found a permanent home for it in her living room above an upright piano. Stately and pensive as ever, Carver stared out inquisitively from his new perch.

In 1991, 30 years after purchasing the portrait with her classmates, Mattie's daughter – me – looked at the mysterious but stately man in the photo while practicing scales on the piano. I had learned about Carver in school as most people do – his many uses for the peanut were touted as his core contributions. I vaguely recall reading the term "crop rotation" in a history chapter about the boll weevil that decimated Southern crops at one point, but I can't say I knew much else.

But on a serendipitous trip to Tuskegee University in 2015 – formerly Tuskegee Institute – where Carver lived until his death in 1943, I visited the Carver Center on campus with my elementary-aged sons. While there, I felt a sense of eerie familiarity. Though I'd never set foot on the campus, it was as if I had been there before. And as I reacquainted myself with his life story and work, it was also as if Carver from above the piano had been with me even before I was conscious of his work.

In 2017, when I came up with the name *Purposescaping* to describe the way forward for coaching clients who had reached a career impasse and wanted to find their way to more fulfilling work, I kept going back to Carver's ideas about rotation and restoration. I'd observed a seasonal and cyclical nature in how my clients were seeking purpose, finding fulfillment, and renewing their drive to succeed. The removal, replacement, and rotation core of Carver's solution emerged again and again as a metaphor for my work.

Purposescaping, I thought, is how we can apply some of George Washington Carver's methods for restoration to human beings. It is a process for bringing people into alignment with a focus on energy-generating activities and energy-generating relationships to restore individuals depleted from burnout.

Carver's organic, conservation-minded approach offered clear solutions to the crisis of depleted soil at a crucial moment in our country's history. It is my opinion that his work is not yet done because it offers a roadmap for how we – worn down by overworking and ravaged by burnout – can potentially restore our depleted selves. In the next chapter we'll explore Purposescaping in depth.

8

Purposescaping

Ever since I was about 11 years old, I have used journaling as a self-reflection and coping tool. My parents had marital problems early, and when they finally began the process of divorcing, I knew how to write well enough to express myself and found that it made me feel better. I would journal about my days, my thoughts, and my feelings. I would wonder about the issues facing my parents; I'd confess my devastation, and I'd detail my loneliness. At the time, therapy was frowned upon in my community, and if it was taken advantage of at all it would have been for the adults, not the children. So aside from my childhood friends who indulged me as much as other children could, I wrote.

A Habit of Self-Reflection

In the process of developing a journaling and writing habit, I naturally became self-reflective. By putting pen to paper regularly, I began to amass a life story that I could read back over, notice themes, and observe patterns. Becoming self-reflective meant that I became a noticer of themes and patterns not only in my own life but in the lives of others.

I can remember as a child looking at adults and families, trying to understand what made things "work." What occupations tended to lead to the type of income that precluded houses in the affluent suburbs? What types of behaviors did I observe from the people who made me feel safe and secure versus fearful? What were the commonalities among the people in my life who seemed "happy" and well adjusted? What did they all have? What did they all do on a regular basis? What were the common themes and common denominators?

I had used these observation skills in my work as a journalist, of course, but as a personal branding coach, they took on new significance for me. I knew enough to know that for most people, there are common threads that have been expressed throughout their lives. But I realized that, for whatever reason, most people weren't in the habit of reflecting on their lives like I was.

So my mission became helping them to see their own themes. It started out with step one of the Package Your Genius framework, a process of focused inquiry that forces them explore the past in terms of activities and people that energized, drained, and provided some sort of value exchange.

In the process of listening, I realized that by hearing their stories I could quickly begin to see their patterns clearly. And by helping them see their patterns, see their stories, and see what the past has to teach them about their lives today, they could get clear on who they really are.

Stop the Guessing Game

When asked about your passions, motivations, and desires, instead of guessing, look over your life. Two things that don't lie are your actions and your energy. So if you're contemplating a new direction, think about what excited you and what drained you about past directions. When you faced a fork in the road and had to make a pivotal choice, did that little voice inside of you say, "I don't know about this," or were you just super excited to go forward even though it didn't make any sense? Your physical and emotional responses to past pivotal moments are yours to access as your personal wisdom.

There's something internal, something inside of us that's always trying to help guide our paths. My work has increasingly become about helping people reconnect with that internal voice, so that they can see the truth of their life.

This whole notion of Purposescaping is about illuminating the path – sweeping the dirt and dust away from your unique path so you can see where it goes. And I believe we all have a map for this path that was encoded in each of us before we were even born.

A Seasonal Framework

Purposescaping is divided into four sections that align with seasonal changes of a temperate climate. I do understand that depending on one's geography, you may live in a tropical, desert, alpine, or even polar climate. But climate-change and extreme climate conditions aside, I personally look to nature for the most infinite wisdom and see parallels that we can learn from and lessons we can apply to the art of living and thriving. You can consider my use of temperate climates an ode to both George Washington Carver's work and to the work of both sets of my grandparents, who at certain points farmed land in the southeastern United States.

Overview

Burnout is caused by multiple misalignments. Misalignments create friction, and friction leaks unnecessary energy. Misalignments create energy leaks that compound over time. Purposescaping solves for misalignment.

Purposescaping is how we apply George Washington Carver's methods of crop rotation to human beings. It is the process of bringing people into alignment with a focus on energy-generating activities and energy-generating relationships to restore individuals depleted from burnout. In short, Purposescaping is crop rotation of the self.

Purposescaping is the act of excavating your purpose, getting to the root of who you are, why you are, what you're passionate about, and how you want to use your gifts and talents in the world before clearing the path to bring your purpose to life.

The Purposescaping Seasons

Winter rest is a time for reflection, assessment, and decisions. Just as certain animals hibernate during the winter months due to food scarcity, and the body rejuvenates during a night of sleep, there are advantages to allowing your purpose time to recharge. Instead of seeing rest as a period of little activity, we know that many essential functions are happening mentally and spiritually during a resting stage. The same way that new buds emerge powerfully after the weather breaks, rest is required to allow you to repeat the Purposescaping cycle with increased vigor. Reflection is required for the best decisions.

Spring planting is the phase in the journey of birthing a dream when big decisions must be made about the direction you'll take, and preparing the environment for success. In spring you commit to a direction for the next several seasons, which is why the work of winter is so important. Planting is about timing, location, focus – all of the important decisions one must make before taking a big leap. How can you be thoughtful about your direction so that you have the highest probability of success?

Summer growth is an active phase where we first get a chance to see whether what we planted took root. Was this a fruitful direction? We see growth and acceleration during this phase. We're not quite at the point of harvesting, but if things stall out during this phase, we won't make it to harvest. Growth is about forward movement, but also about taking care of the new fruits that have begun to show promise – what needs to be weeded out to ensure growth can continue? What nutrients are needed to complete this growth cycle? How can we troubleshoot when problems arise, as they inevitably will?

Fall harvest comes after a period of growth when you will eventually need to harvest a fully grown crop before the weather changes. For people, this could mean getting the most out of an opportunity before a trend changes, or competition catches up, or the economy transitions and demand decreases. As you harvest what's good in the crop, you'll also need to prune away the dead branches – remove what's not working – to ensure the future health of your plants.

The Four Seasons

As I've mentioned throughout, machine mindset has diminished the importance of proper rest. But just a cursory search on the subject as it relates to living beings reveals periodic times of rest built into the natural life cycle.

Many bears hibernate during the winter months, transforming their bodies into a state of extended rest that resembles near-death. During this slumber, their heart rates slow and most of their bodily functions cease. From an evolutionary perspective, they are effectively taking themselves out of the food chain during months when their food sources are scarce. It's a brilliant case of the original strategist – nature – at work.

Yet we don't have to go that far to find examples of strategic rest. While many human beings dismiss the need for sleep, experts say that many important functions are happening during our eight hours of rest. Our bodies are hard at work repairing muscles, regulating our hormones, digesting food, and managing the unseen tasks of our biological lives. Our brains are hard at work too – studies have shown that during sleep, the brain is busy creating new memories, cementing information from earlier in the day, and making new connections between old and new information. From an intellectual perspective, the benefits of rest are clear: you can't fully "harvest" the work of the day until you give your body time to rest.

Winter Evaluation

Pruning is an important part of the post-harvest phase because you can experience growth in your business, growth in your platform, and growth in your ideas and what people believe about you. You can grow your career and still end up where it doesn't feel like a perfect fit, or certain aspects of what you're doing can take off whether or not it was what you originally intended.

Or perhaps something you pursued in the past worked for that time, but now it's time to do something different. Sometimes you have to take time to prune away the things that are no longer serving you. Sometimes you have to admit to yourself that certain things don't bring you joy anymore. Sometimes you must realize that there are things that you need to delegate in order to get to your next level. So this part of the harvest is about being honest about the things that do not serve you and removing the excess.

How do you know when to start that pruning process? Once you've given something an ample chance to grow, it's time to evaluate what's working, what's not working, what you can keep, and what must change.

For example, if you decide to start your business or write your book and after two weeks of working hard on it and you see zero traction, you let it go. Did you give it the time needed? Whether you're starting your business, writing your book, or pivoting into a new industry, prepare to put in a lot of work during the planting and growth phases. It won't always be quick and certainly not easy. If you're starting out in a brand-new direction and you don't have a reputation as an author or as a businessperson, your planting and growth phases may be longer than future phases. It depends on what purpose you're birthing, but before you prune, give whatever you're attempting to grow ample time and energy before you give up on it.

Planting

Before you choose a path or start building your brand, a lot of pre-work needs to happen. The planting phase is about getting your mind, environment, and spirit fortified for the process of growth.

Preparing the Ground

In every journey, there are universal blocks that spring up and universal challenges that are going to threaten your progress. Your fears will haunt you most deeply when it's time to start something new. But the beauty of fears is that everyone has them. During the planting process, my goal is to help you recognize universal themes that are keeping you from going after your calling and show you how other people have experienced the same things, so you don't internalize them.

In understanding what will come up, you can depersonalize and realize there's nothing "wrong" with you: you're not broken. This is just what happens whenever someone is about to start that new business, become more visible through speaking, or write that book. These are things that come up for everyone. And so if you can see it, name it, and understand it, when it comes up for you, my hope is that you'll be ready.

Going after our dreams is really a mental game. If you don't believe that you can do it, if you're not strong enough and ready to combat fear and all the things that are going to come up for you, you're already at a disadvantage.

Cracking Open the Seed

The process of a seed becoming a plant is not easy. In that period before it sprouts and becomes a plant, the seed has to go from a smooth, contained entity to a broken case that cracks open to release what is inside. That's kind of what happens when you begin the growth phase of your purpose. You have to crack open before you can grow.

The "cracking open" is you. Because when you finally make the decision to take a step and do this, it's going to hurt. It's going to surprise you, it's going to break your shell, and it's going to expose you. It's going to be uncomfortable.

Nurturing the Invisible

Just as with the seed, after you crack open you must continue to nurture the exponential growth that is taking place underground.

After a planter finishes tilling the earth, putting out seed, they continue to water and tend to the invisible – they know that to support all of the hard work that is happening just beneath the surface of the soil, they must continue to nurture what they can't see just yet.

Understand that in that fragile period after you plant your dream but just before you can see any evidence of it coming to life, growth is happening. So remember to nurture the invisible by taking care of yourself, taking care of your mind, and putting yourself in the position where your environment will also nurture your movements, your gifts, your ideas, your actions.

That means intentionally staying away from the naysayers and the people who are going to discourage you. That means setting up the most ideal situation for growth.

During the growth phase, nurturing your dream means protecting it in its fragile state. Because we all know that you can throw a seed down on a patch of dirt, but if the soil isn't right and it doesn't get enough sunlight and water, nothing's going to happen.

Growth

This is the first phase of traction. It's the first time we begin to see the initial results of moving forward in your purpose. So in the first stage of planting, you may be thinking, getting your thoughts together, making the decision about the particular dream you will pursue, and taking those first initial steps. During the growth phase, our ideas have taken root and we begin to see the first seedlings begin to sprout.

Experimentation

The growth phase is also about experimentation. It's about looking at clues from your past to see where you get the most traction, where you get your energy, what excites you about your work and your life, so you can begin to create those kinds of ideal circumstances intentionally. Because when you are energized and excited, those are periods that you are operating in your purpose.

At this point, you've had some time to think about who you are and what you want, and maybe now you're taking those first steps to get some traction. So that might look a few different ways. For example, if your goal is to write a book, your first steps may be to write your main outline, create a daily writing schedule, and let your accountability partner know that you're writing a book to make it real for yourself.

Commit

Growth is also about commitment because to get to a place of harvest, you must commit to work on what you've chosen to do. After you decide during the planting phase and you have your plan, you must act – consistently.

But along the way, you will be challenged and you will stumble. When you're actually doing the work, you'll be tempted by distractions, comparison, and doubt. You may look to the left or the right and see what other people are doing. You will wonder if other people like what you're doing and you'll doubt your resolve to do the thing you set out to do in the first place.

Be Visible

Growth is also about visibility and, to some degree, vulnerability. You've released whatever you've created into the world, so you are going to face the issues that come with that. Now you'll be subjected to both praise and criticism as others become more involved. After you commit and start putting yourself out there, people will know what you're doing, and it's not a secret anymore.

During growth, there is movement. It's not just about ideas; it's not just about preparation. It's about moving forward with your ideas and sharing them in some way with the world. Growth is about doing the work and releasing your gift.

Harvest

Once you've successfully planted the seed, nurtured the seed, and had a chance to observe the first evidence of growth, at some point you can step back and evaluate your progress.

Know When to Pick the Plant

In the traditional planting cycle, harvest time is the period of the year when the farmer picks the crops at the point of maturity; they have reached a final stage of growth and are now ready to be picked, eaten, or taken to market. But it's important to pick the crop lest it remain on the vine too long and rot.

So it's important to stop and harvest what you've done, which means celebrating the progress you've made and evaluating the good and the bad of the process.

Celebration

Many people make the mistake of never stopping to celebrate the accomplishment of birthing a dream. Even if you write a book, publish it, and only sell 10 copies, the fact that you finished a book is an achievement to celebrate. As you continue on your journey, you will go on to evaluate what went well (finishing) and what didn't go so well (perhaps marketing) and tweak your plan for the next cycle. But failing to stop and celebrate completion is a grave mistake.

Even if it has taken you a decade to finally start, finishing is an accomplishment to be celebrated. In your celebration, you give yourself needed fuel for the next cycle of Purposescaping.

The Wrong Harvest

The importance of the previous two phases becomes clear during the harvest. You must do the work of identifying where to place your focus – what to grow – or like many people you'll find yourself harvesting something that you don't even want!

Unfortunately, that happens a lot. Many people sink a lot of time, effort, energy, and money into growing something, and when they harvest it they realize they don't even like it. They're miserable because the harvest doesn't make them happy. This is why it's important to do the work of self-exploration, because if you decide on a direction that is inauthentic, you will end up with something that you don't even want.

If you're not being honest, and you're not doing the work of digging to find out what lights you up, what your consistent patterns have been throughout your life, you may very well end up with something that looks very good, and is maybe even very profitable, but it's just not what you want. It doesn't make you happy, and you're still not fulfilled. And I think, ultimately, the goal of Purposescaping is to find your most purposeful, fulfilling work.

Can your most purposeful work change over time? Absolutely! But that's why there is a process – you just start it all over again. It's a cycle, just like in nature.

The Work of Winter Rest and Decisions

Because this is a book about burnout and restoration, a discussion of winter is critical. In Chapter 4, I talked about how repeatedly skipping winter does immense damage and leads to burnout. Now I want to share what leaning into winter looks like.

The Work of Winter

Just as a plant may bud, bloom, wilt, and rest, the work of winter is centered on the phase of resting – a time to pause for a period of dormancy so you can reflect on what's working, decide on a direction, and plan the work of the next season. It's a time to evaluate current assets, change out tools, plow under the soil, and release what no longer serves your goals.

Winter Evaluation and Decisions

Winter is about evaluation. You need a season of evaluation and assessment so you know whether your efforts during the previous seasons are yielding any fruit, and if you should change your methods, decrease your intensity, or double down on what's working.

Winter is also about decisions, which are necessary if you want to move with purpose.

The first type of decision to make is about the crops. Do you want to take the "crops" of your past into the spring planting season? Do you want to increase the amount you plant? Do you need to move your crops to different parts of the field (try a new approach)? Or do you want to try something new altogether?

The next type of decision to make is about tools. During the busy seasons of growth and harvest, you may have experienced mechanical breakdowns, or observed parts that need to be replaced. Now is the time to make those replacements and upgrades. Note that you may have outgrown the machinery of this season and can't take it with you into the spring. So now's the time to evaluate whether the machinery you have still fits the type of job you have to do and, if not, where will you upgrade and with what? Where do *you* need to upgrade?

Rest is not really rest. It's like taking vitamins that are necessary for optimal growth.

Winter is also a season for "plowing under" – the act of turning the ground over to give it air, refresh it, and bring stagnant soil up to the surface. What aspects of your life and purpose do you need to plow under, bring to the surface, and potentially give new life?

Winter is a season for release. What isn't working?

Winter is necessary; this is not an optional season. There's a lot going on underground. But also, the soil needs a break. You need a break. You cannot bloom year-round.

What to Release

When it comes to deciding what to release during winter, we can start with your energy. What work and projects energized you and drained you over the last 12 months?

- What situations energized and drained you?
- Which people energized you? Which drained you?

- What did you get right this year? What were your wins?
- What will you change? What can you celebrate?
- What were the major wins, milestones, and key moments of the past year?
- What is your vision for next year?

While the growth phase may be intoxicating, growth cannot be your only speed, nor can you exist only in that season. You must alternate periods of growth with rest in order to continue to produce a healthy harvest.

The Work of Spring Planting

Just like the planter, you must identify a safe place to plant and then prepare the ground for the seed. This means identifying the right patch of soil that will allow for just the right amount of light to hit whatever you're growing, just the right amount of rain to discourage flooding if that's an issue for the crop you're planting, access to abundant minerals, and protection from any potential predators.

Similarly, your dreams require that you ensure the environment is nurturing and that you're planting on fertile soil. This not only means the state of your life or the soil, but it also relates to timing, the people you have around you, and any other parts of the environment because they can all affect your dream either positively or negatively.

Before planters plant, they seek the best location that is available and conducive to the growth of their plants. They also make sure to plant in the proper season so the plants have time to sprout, grow, and bear fruit before the winter. Just as the planter considers time and place, you must also consider the timing of your movements and actions.

Are you ready for the next season of growth? Do you have ample time to support a burgeoning dream – one that is growing and needs support, nutrients, and attention from you?

Even if a planter plants a seed in fertile ground with all of the right things, if they plant the seed too early or too late, nothing will grow. Or worse, it will grow but never reach maturation before being snuffed out by the first frost. You must pay attention to timing, to yourself, and hone your internal compass to know when you have the time to give to this new endeavor.

The work of spring planting is also deciding the direction of growth. Before a seed can sprout and become a plant, the planter must decide what seed to plant. As for you, this time is important and you must make critical decisions about how you will spend your precious time and what you will nurture.

Many people make the mistake of not considering what they want to plant before striking out to nurture something and watch it grow. That's why you find people who are outwardly successful, but inside they are unfulfilled and unhappy despite everything pointing to the opposite. Because they did not sufficiently take time to decide what they wanted to plant, they ended up tending to whatever plants grew on their plot of land. So successful spring planting entails being intentional about what plant you want to tend, what you want to nurture, and ultimately what you want to see grow and bear fruit in your life.

After you've made decisions and prepared the ground, it is time to activate your plan. This phase is fragile and one of new beginnings. You must give tremendous energy to a seed for it to get what it needs to crack open, take root, and begin the process of growing into a seedling or young plant.

A newly sprouted seed needs plenty of sunlight and water and lots of tender loving care, just as you will need as you are in these first fragile steps of setting out on your new path. You will have to be vigilant about curating the most optimal environment in order to succeed. While everyone is different and some people need more nurturing or less, it is up to you to learn your limitations, your triggers, and your requirements for success during this phase. Once you understand what you need to optimize your gifts, it is your responsibility to intentionally curate those exact conditions for the cultivation of your dream.

As you plant and water your dreams, you will need to think about the people who surround you because their words and energy can be positive or negative and can either build you up or break you down.

Depending upon how susceptible you are to outside influence, again you must know yourself; this is the time to seek out like-minded individuals and supportive communities or other groups of people who are walking in the same direction. It may also be time to avoid those who discourage you, discount you, or have limited information on the path you wish to take. You want to find as many positive influences for yourself as possible. This could include seeking out books, videos, a mentor or coach, classes, and other things that will pour into you, feed you, and nurture you as you tend to your growing dream.

In short, ask yourself what input you need to get the desired outcome. If anything is not moving toward your end goal, don't hesitate to remove it from your environment. Or should you find yourself deficient in a certain area, swiftly find resources that can nurture that deficiency.

The Work of Summer Growth

During summer growth, the time of decision-making is over; it is time to leap forth into action and begin making moves on the decisions you made during winter rest and spring planting.

You have created life where there was nothing before. You've experienced almost a full cycle of bringing something to fruition. At this point you want to keep your dream going so you will require yourself to keep going.

Growth does not stop when the first leaf sprouts or when the first piece of fruit becomes ripe. It is a continual process that you will need to commit to if you want to continue to see fruits. As any gardener knows, you must take care of the plants if you want them to continue to prosper. And although you may have planted countless seeds during the spring planting, not every one will turn into a plant. Furthermore, some of the plants that grow will die and you will have to accept that although they sprouted, they weren't strong enough to survive the season. Some may succumb to infestations, insects, severe storms, or drought. Even when you start with the perfect conditions, those conditions may change.

The same environment and conditions that grow healthy plants also encourage the growth of other plants we may consider to be weeds. For example, your ambition during the growth phase may grow delicious fruits of success; however, the fertilizer and rainwater that fed the growth of your healthy fruit-bearing plant also fed the growth of weeds and pests. Good growing conditions support growth, after all.

Your ambition may create external success in your career, a new business, or an intellectual project like a book. But it may also come at the expense of your relationships, time with your children, or your marriage.

Your ambition, which is an essential nutrient for growth, has a shadow side that could manifest in arrogance, or serve to amplify parts of yourself that you would rather leave in the dark.

When the right set of environments conspire together for the right length of time, your seed will grow strong and healthy, and if you're lucky your plant will bear some fruit.

Growth will reveal what was strong enough to stand and survive.

The Work of Fall Harvest

At this point it is time to harvest the hard work of bringing something to life.

Purposescaping teaches self-actualization through the seasons. It's all about clearing a pathway to your purpose. That language is intentional – we're clearing a path to something that has been there all along. It may be overgrown, it may be hidden, but the path is there. The purpose is there. I believe that wholeheartedly.

The concept of crop rotation is key. You can't plant the same thing over and over on the same plot of land. You can't do the same thing over and over as it pertains to your goals, dreams, and purpose – you have to explore the different facets of yourself, stretch yourself and learn more about how you tick. Time changes all things – even you.

There is no specific deadline to harvest your crop, but you don't have forever. Even though you've put in the hard work to plant and grow and protect your crop from predators, you can't leave it in the ground forever. You have to put it to use before it expires.

Just as there are threats to growth, there are threats to fully grown harvests. Practically speaking, I see aging and time as my own personal threat because I know I won't always have the energy and youth to do many of the things I dream up as this version of myself. Another practical threat to a harvest could be physical health, available free time, or financial resources to commit to exploring your purpose.

Don't rest on your harvest (laurels). Be present to your success, but always keep an eye toward the future and use any season of success to look for clues about what you may want to do in the future.

No Season Is Wasted

It took me a long time to learn that just as there are seasons in nature, there are seasons of purpose. If you think about winter, spring, summer, and fall, it's easy to see what's happening in nature during any given season.

The ground rests in winter, blossoms to life during spring, matures during summer, and finally generates a harvest during the fall, before fading away and settling in for another period of rest.

Most of us don't question the changes happening on the trees and with the animals – we've come to expect those changes, and even may say things like "everything in its season." But when it comes to our own lives, careers, relationships, and businesses, I've noticed we aren't generally so understanding.

One mantra I took up a few years ago was "no flower blooms year-round." Though the less poetic truth is that most flowers don't bloom year-round, there are actually a few that produce blooms all year.

In the same vein, I recently read a powerful quote on Instagram, which was attributed to Maya Angelou: "Every storm runs out of rain."

The same is true for us.

I don't know about you, but during periods of success, especially in business, I used to want them to go on forever. I'd want to stay in the harvest phase year-round because harvesting is often so much more fun than the work of preparing the ground, planting, and tending to healthy growth. And when harvest time would inevitably end, I would be disappointed and almost feel a sense of failure because the boom time was over.

But I eventually realized that life, business, and relationships, like pretty much everything under the sun, all move in cycles. And while the harvest may feel great in the moment, a perpetual season of harvest just isn't sustainable. You actually *need* those other seasons to make the harvest all it can be. They're not just nice-to-haves – they're necessities.

Can you see how no season is wasted? You can't expect a revenue windfall during the harvest season if you didn't plant or create anything noteworthy during spring.

But this philosophy doesn't just apply to building a career or business, although that is what my company has focused on over the last 10 years. It also applies to building a family, developing your spirituality, or putting creative work into the world.

For example, I have two teenaged children. I remember the first few years of my kids' lives being entrenched in the planting phase. It seemed like I was planting, planting, planting for years until they transitioned into a season of growth. Now I'm in a clear season of harvest where I can see the rewards of the groundwork I laid during those early years, both academically and emotionally – those seeds have not only sprouted into strong plants, but they're bearing unmistakable fruit.

As my teens transition into young adults, I'm taking time to reflect on who they are and who I am as a mother – what I would have done differently up to this point as a parent, what worked well, what I've learned about them, and what I'll change moving forward.

While these "seasons" weren't three months like a cycle of farming might be – for them, I would say each season has lasted about three years instead – each season has been necessary.

When they were younger, I didn't have the benefit of hindsight to understand how those grueling planting years were temporary and would give way to a new season, or that they were a setup to an era of harvest. But having experienced a full cycle of parenting I'm even more convicted in the validity of this concept of Purposescaping and I'm certain that no season is wasted.

I can point to countless other examples in my own life, as I'm sure you can in yours.

For many people, the year 2020 presented challenges and opportunities to prioritize rest and reflection. So many people reported feeling burnt out prior to the coronavirus pandemic. Why? Because they had likely been pushing themselves to stay in a growth and harvest season when their bodies, minds, and spirits needed to stop and rest. And nature has a way of course correcting.

A season doesn't have to last three months – one season in your career may last one quarter, while a season in your marriage may last two years – but the idea is to zero in on the cadence that is naturally occurring in whatever part of your life you choose to focus on.

Instead of considering yourself behind in one aspect of your life, or beating yourself up as high achievers are prone to do when they haven't been able to do more, or nothing seems to be "happening" – consider that you may be in a season of reflection and rest instead of a season of creativity and planting. Or you may be in a season of steady maturation and growth that will set you up for that incredible season of harvest.

Wherever you are, remember it's a necessary phase in the cycle – no season is wasted.

Optimal Growing Conditions

We all have a different recipe that allows us to grow and thrive at our best. A part of Purposescaping – just like landscaping – is getting clear on what growing conditions *you* specifically need to be your best.

Just like plants come with care instructions – one may need full sunlight and regular water, while another requires moderate shade and drier soil – if you fail to follow the instructions you'll notice the plant starts to talk back to you. It may wilt or droop, its colors may fade, and eventually it may wither and die. I know I have overwatered my fair share of succulents, even though it felt like watering was the right thing to do.

Yet when a plant's optimal growing conditions are met, it thrives and you almost have to prune it back to contain the growth.

Why would we be any different? As living things, human beings all have a unique imprint we came to earth with – one unlike anyone else's. We all have an optimal set of growing conditions that, when met, allow us to thrive. Yet many of us fail to examine our own ideal growing criteria and assume we need the same thing as the next person.

Not true.

By way of example, I have personally enjoyed creating regular content my whole life. In the last 15 years or so, that's taken the shape of me publishing a blog, a newsletter, and most recently a podcast. I used to fill my journals with my thoughts and ideas – and I still do to some extent. But when I discovered the act of publishing some of those ideas via a blog and then via a podcast, I realized that the full cycle of having an insight, packaging it for others, sharing it, and receiving feedback was what really lights me up.

There's a rhythm to creating content on a regular basis that really fuels me. It's like full sunlight or the right amount of water – when I'm doing it, I thrive creatively. I notice other things in my life start to fall into place. I'm making mental connections, I'm getting creative ideas, I'm growing my audience and even adding new clients.

But more importantly, I feel like *myself*. I'm operating in my zone because I am taking time to give myself what I need to be my best.

Another one of my conditions for optimal growth? Regular time in nature. This is something I got quite a bit of growing up in the South. I didn't realize how much I needed it until I began a regular practice of nature hiking and forest bathing several years ago.

With schedule and routine changes due to the pandemic, that forest time was put on hold. And I can definitely feel the absence. It's not so much that I withered away without it, but I notice I'm not as vibrant as I was when it was a regular part of my life.

So regular content creation and time in nature are two of my optimal growing conditions. Neither of these are deal breakers; I can live without them. But I'm at *my best* when they're a regular part of my life.

I find that many of us know our optimal growing criteria, but we don't always give ourselves permission to indulge. Add in the fact that not having those criteria met won't kill us, they're the first on the chopping block when our schedules get hectic or our budgets tighten up. But if we're going to truly clear a path to our purpose and achieve the highest version of ourselves, we have to move beyond the bare minimum and step into the optimal environment so we can truly thrive.

How can you understand your own optimal growing criteria? Here are a few questions to help you figure it out:

- Is there a practice you had earlier in your life that you really enjoyed? What happened to it?
- What season do you blossom in?
- What ingredients do you need to be your best?
- What's your rhythm for productivity?
- How can you tell you need to rest?
- How much social engagement do you need? How much solitude?
- When you feel most at peace, what are you generally doing? Who is around?
- When you feel most productive, what have you been doing? What are the common denominators?
- When you find yourself least susceptible to stress, what supports do you have in place?
- When you feel most joyful, what is usually involved?

Purposescaping – the art of clearing a path to your purpose – is about radical self-discovery. You probably study the needs of others whom you care about the most. Now it's time to do a deep dive on yourself and what you need to be your absolute best.

Myleik's Journey

Myleik Teele, whom you first met in Chapter 4, has been on what I consider an ultimate journey of Purposescaping. Her journey is a great example of the seasonal nature of success – even when you find tremendous success in one area, it doesn't mean there's nothing left to accomplish.

"I did something, and I did something well, and I'm not doing that anymore," she told me of her business success.

She says she is most excited about the opportunity to be a beginner again and is embracing the idea of starting over, making mistakes, and trying new things. While many people know her from beauty subscription company Curlbox or her podcast, she says she's now exploring her passion for working with people to help them unlock their gifts and build the lives they want.

"I even say this to people when I'm doing my podcast. My answers are not your answers. They are just a way, an alternative view on things. But how can I work with you to get you living in your truth and maybe help you with the resources to help you get there?" That's her current mission. Sometimes people just don't know the right person or who to turn to for answers. She'd like to fill that gap.

"I think sometimes we think that it's harder than it is, but the truth of the matter is that most of us just don't have the access or haven't been exposed or have been too embarrassed to ask for help or don't even know that help exists."

When she started her online mom group Myleik & Mommas, Myleik discovered that many mothers wouldn't have asked for certain resources, simply because they didn't know they were available. This realization has driven her to spend more time focusing on helping others access the support they need on the parenting journey. While she still loves working on business ventures and may help others with theirs, she is particularly enthusiastic about bringing people together and guiding them toward success.

She sees herself as a lighthouse, guiding people to the right places and connections that enable them to live their best lives. She wants to continue this work, helping more individuals unlock their potential.

Especially when she travels, she finds herself naturally helping people unlock new opportunities. "Every time I would go somewhere I would just be doing that. I came home from a trip with someone and it was like, Oh my God, I helped them unlock all these different things. And I said to my partner, I want to do more of that. I want to do more of that because I feel like sometimes people are just waiting in the wrong line. They're just heading in the wrong direction."

Graduating from a Season

As Teele showed us, it's okay to let go of a season, even if that season has served you.

Purposescaping is largely about learning how to read the signs and answer the call for your life. Yet what happens when you hear the call for something different but ignore it because (1) you're comfortable where you are and don't want to be inconvenienced by the unknown and you don't want to be a beginner again, and (2) you're proud of the level you're on? You worked hard to get there, and it feels like you'll be "throwing away" all the hard work it took to arrive.

But even when the season you're in has served you well, it's okay to let go of it if you're being called to something higher.

I've seen this play out in numerous ways. I've heard from colleagues who consciously uncoupled and left marriages that no longer served them but were able to remain friends. Things didn't have to get to a breaking point; it just wasn't working anymore. And even though there was a lot that could hold them together – in one case, property, joint assets, and three kids; in another case property, assets, and over a decade of friendship – they didn't cling to the past just because there was something there. They answered the call of a new season, and so far it's working out.

As a matter of fact, I have *never* heard someone say they took a leap of faith and answered internal, God-given direction and lived to regret it.

Have you?

Our brains will trick us into believing that what we have now is as good as it's going to get. But what if there is more? Actually, there is no what if – there is so much more available to us than we can even imagine. Imagining more is actually the first step to being able to notice what's there for us when it walks into our lives.

Here are five signs you're in an expired season and it's time for you to let go.

Coasting

I've literally said to myself "I'm coasting off of a past version of myself." I know I'm in an expired season when I'm not working hard to grow. I'm not innovating. I'm not looking for new solutions. I'm just gliding off what's worked in the past. And yes, that yields some good stuff, even revenue, but it's nowhere near what I could have if I let go of what feels comfortable and lean into what's beckoning me.

No Curiosity

You have no questions because you feel that there's nothing new to learn. If you are no longer looking for new ways to grow because you're being stretched, you've likely stayed on this level too long.

Boredom

You're bored because you've outgrown an old version of yourself. That old self may have served you quite well, made you a lot of money, won you accolades in an industry you don't care about anymore. But if you're feeling antsy and wondering what's next, you already know this season has expired.

Unimpressed

You're unimpressed with yourself. This is true for so many of my clients. Like them, you are so impressive to other people – you look like a success to other people but you don't *feel* like a success to yourself because you know you've yet to scratch the surface of your capabilities. You're doing what you can do, but not what you were born to do, and even if you can't put your finger on what you ultimately should be doing, you know that there's got to be more than this.

Anxiety

Thinking about your next level gives you anxiety. You're scared to answer the call because you're low-key afraid of your own power. You have never put it in fifth gear before and that unknown realm frightens you. What if you can't hack it on the next level? What if there's more to do and learn than you anticipated and you're not up for the challenge? If you're having thoughts like this, you already know. You're in an expired season.

Now, I'm not a professional at switching seasons. I naturally get caught up in sunk cost bias and hold on to things longer than they serve me, which is why I can call it out! For those who don't know, sunk cost bias is the idea that the more time, money, or other resources invested in something, the harder it is to let it go. You desperately want it to work, almost to prove yourself right, or at least not wrong for sinking so many of your resources into it. This is why you see people staying in marriages for years even when they're not happy, or sticking with a strategy that is clearly not working because they've dumped so much time and money into it.

At this point in my life, nothing I've had the courage to let go of has been better than what was waiting for me on the other side.

What about you? Are you in a season that has served you well, but you know – even in a tiny way – that you need to let go of it? Letting go may allow you to make room for something different, for something better, for something you *really* want.

Your Next Season

I'm a huge fan of the idea of "living within your means." Financially, this is being sensible enough not to spend what you don't have. If you don't have it in the bank or can't reliably project that it's coming in, don't stretch yourself to buy things you'll have to pay back on credit or you'll end up digging yourself a financial hole. Your means are your means. Stick to them.

That works financially. But in other areas of our life, sometimes we need to live outside of our means, because we are living too small. We're thinking too small. Let's call these our spiritual means.

It makes sense for us to live within our financial means because we can see how getting ahead of ourselves can land us in a world of debt. But living within our spiritual means requires us to rely only on what we can see in the now. If we have an idea, we have to be able to see the pathway and have all of our questions answered before we're brave enough to take a chance. For most people, there will never be enough answers to satisfy our doubts. So we'll stay where we are. Coasting.

The danger of choosing to live within our spiritual means is that we don't allow ourselves to expand enough to make it to the next level that was already promised to us – and we know it was promised because the call keeps beckoning us.

When it's time to envision something bigger for your life, you may not know how you're going to get there but the important thing is to allow the energy of that desire to come in. Allow yourself to see it, allow yourself to dream it, allow yourself to visualize yourself living it. Allow yourself to admit that this is really what you want!

If you think of the stories of people who inspire you, most of them have identified a certain something that is unique about themselves – a certain something they can bring to the forefront and use to dominate whatever industry they're in or do something truly remarkable. But beyond that focus and a ton of hard work, it all boils down to the fact that they decided to go for whatever it is that at first seemed impossible. They decided to answer the call.

Why not you?

To answer the call is to live beyond your spiritual means, to accept an invitation to move higher in your own evolution. In Purposescaping, I teach a principle called "spiraling up," which means taking everything you've learned about yourself on one level and refining it so you have an even narrower, more focused iteration of your calling on the next level. Imagine a pyramid that gets narrower and narrower as you approach the top. That's the path to your purpose. And as you spiral up to each subsequent level, the levels get more focused.

As you "spiral up" enough times over the course of your life, you find yourself walking in a version of your purpose that only you can occupy. But the first step of getting to that hyper-focused version of the purpose that was designed specifically for you and only you is essentially a faith walk. It's answering a call when you're not sure where the call is leading you – where the journey is taking you, whether or not this crazy idea of yours is going to work.

I can't tell you whether anything you do or anything you try will work. But I can tell you that a part of the journey to clearing a pathway to what you were meant to do with your life comes in large part from acting, moving, making mistakes, learning from those mistakes, refining, recrafting, eliminating the excess, and pruning away the branches that are dead and stalling your future growth.

Remember, your next level was already promised to you. How do you know? You know it was promised to you and only you because it keeps calling you and only you. No one else can hear your call. No one else can see your path with the clarity you see it. But nobody else can validate it for you. No one else can confirm it. No one else can tell you they see what you see.

And I believe you see it. I know you do. You just may not be allowing yourself to answer it by taking that first step because it feels almost like a mirage. You're afraid you're stepping out over a cliff into nothingness because you have no proof there's solid ground to support your next step. You're trying to live within your means by sticking to what you know.

And yet the call keeps calling, daring you to evolve.

More often than not, your purpose will call you to an unknown place, and if this resonates with you, it's time to live beyond your means.

Why You Have Muscle Memory

Muscle memory is defined as "the ability to reproduce a particular movement without conscious thought, acquired as a result of frequent repetition of that movement."

According to Wikipedia, "When a movement is repeated over time, a long-term muscle memory is created for that task, eventually allowing it to be performed without conscious effort. This process decreases the need for attention and creates maximum efficiency within the motor and memory systems. Examples of muscle memory are found in many everyday activities that become automatic and improve with practice, such as riding a bicycle, typing on a keyboard, entering a PIN, playing a musical instrument, poker, martial arts, or even dancing."

But beyond riding a bicycle (you never forget, right?) or playing a musical instrument, there is a degree of muscle memory involved in doing the activities required to build your personal brand in a public way. I'm reminded of a time I spoke on a stage during a period of intense personal grief, in the wake of my father's death. Although I can't recall anything I said that day, whatever I said was enough to catch the attention of new clients and win the respect of corporate sponsors.

If you're nervous about putting yourself out there, I remind you that you've already done the work. Lean on your muscle memory – your hard-won expertise – and don't put pressure on yourself to know everything and be brilliant in the moment. You can access the lessons you've learned along the way whenever you need them. They're there for you.

Exercise: Using the Story Pyramid

Finding Your Leadership North Star: Radical Self-Discovery and Your Formula for Success and Leadership

Use the Purposescaping story pyramid to connect the dots in your career story, uncover your common themes, and understand the major patterns and stories of your life:

- Understand your underlying success story – how you've always summoned change in the past
- Come face to face with your leadership genius
- Get back in touch with your authenticity and bring your full self to work
- Create a rubric for decision-making

Use this signature Purposescaping coaching process to answer this question: What are my career seasons telling me? Use the story pyramid to connect the dots in your career story, uncover your common themes over time, get back in touch with your authenticity, and bring your full self to work.

Deepen Your Purposescaping Work with Story Pyramids

Think back on your childhood, adolescence, early adulthood, early career, and mid-career. Think back on the first phase of your business, the middle point, and your most recent evolution. Think back on your first clients and services as well as the clients you serve and services you offer now. At every major level, there's a story.

Step One: Pick five. Pick a "container" that has five distinct sections or periods. The container can be time based, as in the last five years of your career or the last five articles you wrote and really enjoyed. Or it can be something like your five most energizing career projects to date. These don't need to be paid or work experiences. You may even want to go down memory lane and look at **five major phases of your life**: early childhood, adolescence, college years/early 20s/young adulthood, mid-career, and now.

Reflect on one of the following, and put them in the pyramid beginning with the oldest item at the bottom and the most recent item at the top:
- Five major life stages
- Your last five roles
- Your five best clients
- Your last five services/programs.

Step Two: Note what energized you about each project and make a list of active phrases. Feel free to explore artistic and creative pursuits, any volunteer work, hobbies, community work, friendships, and so on. **But follow the energy** – what can you vividly recall feeling energized by? For example, you might list working with complete autonomy, working on the marketing team, or presenting on stage before dozens of your peers. Don't worry about repeating yourself if the things that energized you show up on multiple parts of the pyramid.

Step Three: List what problems it energized you to solve in each project and make a list of active phrases. For example, you might list helping young people better communicate, bringing order and efficiency to chaos, or motivating the team to keep moving.

Step Four: Note the themes you observe. What audience showed up more than once? What problem were you energized to solve again and again? Sample themes could look like amplifying marginalized voices, making complex ideas easy to understand, creating processes to organize chaos into order, or getting major projects unstuck.

To find your message, reflect on each level categorically by examining the common themes in what energized you, where others extracted value, and in your narrative – on each level.

The beauty of the pyramid exercise is that it allows you to see how your perspective on working has changed – or remained steady – over time. You can see both your evolution and the stable aspects of your character more clearly. Your abilities to plan, create, grow, and achieve depend on each other. Each new season builds on the last in some way.

When you're working in your purpose, you can spot recurring themes, even if those themes show up differently. Finding the common thread on the story pyramid gives you insight into who you are and shows you who you've always been, which can help you find your focus and make decisions.

What natural cycles can you observe in your life and career? What season are you in?

Key Insights

- Purposescaping is how we apply George Washington Carver's methods of crop rotation to human beings.
- Purposescaping is the process of bringing people into alignment with a focus on **energy-generating activities** and **energy-generating relationships** to restore individuals depleted from burnout.
- Purposescaping is crop rotation of the self.
- Burnout is caused by multiple misalignments. Misalignments create friction and friction leaks unnecessary energy. Misalignments create energy leaks that compound over time. Purposescaping solves for misalignment.
- Operating in your purpose is kind of like driving a car – you can still drive it when it is out of alignment, but something feels off. The friction that creates energy leaks comes at a cost and wears you down over time.
- Do more in alignment – not less – to fix burnout.
- Dormant doesn't mean dead. When an animal is dormant, its normal physical functions are suspended or slowed down for a period of time, as if in a deep sleep. Too often, we mistake dormancy for being dead. People, projects, ideas, books, and relationships require tremendous energy to bring to life, but at times will also require significant amounts of stillness and rest to regain their full potential. If you're discouraged by what seems like a lack of progress, find yourself moving slower than your typical pace, or perhaps you're not seeing as much movement as you've seen in the past, and in a certain area of your life, know that this is not always a sign for you to give up. This could simply be your time to regenerate, and let the lessons of this season take root, your time to rest before the next cycle of growth begins.

* * *

The premise of the book is basically that burnout is caused by a series of misalignments. These misalignments go against our natural inclinations, creating friction that leads to energy leaks. As these energy leaks compound, we experience a sense of burnout brought on by having to account for so much friction.

In addition, since we are not allowing ourselves access to the things that generate energy for us – the aligned things – we miss out on the chance to naturally fuel our tanks.

I believe that by reducing the friction of misalignment, and by allowing ourselves to partake in the energy-generating activities, work, and relationships that are unique to us, we will generate the energy we need to exit burnout.

What follows is a series of descriptions that, while not conclusive, are the areas I have found most of my clients struggling with across the board. I will share a simple framework you can use to make changes in one or more of these areas. This framework applies to all five areas of self, ambition, time, nervous system, and connections. It is a cognitive behavioral therapy process used by psychologists and therapists to help clients make behavior changes.

First, you want to become present and aware in terms of where you are right now. What is the current state of things? How do you normally react and respond when it comes to your time, ambition, self-knowledge, relationships, and the like? Do you make time to prioritize these things, or do you generally put something else above these critical areas? If you don't prioritize an area, ask yourself why. In this way, you can understand the truth and take yourself off autopilot. What is your assumption about how you relate to this area? For example, do you tell yourself you don't have time to meditate? Or perhaps you tell yourself that others don't have time to hang out and spend quality time with you? Are these assumptions true? Once you investigate the truth of your default thinking, it will be easier for you to take yourself off autopilot.

Second, ask yourself what is behind your standard way of thinking. How did these ideas emerge? How did these habits and patterns form?

Is this something you've always done since childhood or watched your parents do? Have you always prioritized connection in favor of working long hours to earn more money? Did you watch parents prioritize connection at the peril of financial abundance? Where did your way of working come from? Once you understand what is driving your default, you can disrupt your programming.

Third, realign yourself by getting to the heart of what you are truly hungry for. Everyone is different so only you can answer this question. What are you hungry for when it comes to your relationship with yourself? What are you hungry for when it comes to your career and work? What are you hungry for when it comes to the time to do things? What do you wish you had more time to do? What are you hungry for when it comes to stillness and the ability to heal your nervous system? What do your body and nervous system crave? What are you hungry for in terms of connection? Where are you lonely? Who do you miss?

Once you're clear on your answers in each area, decide on one or two changes that can help you get those hungers satiated.

9 | Restore Self

The first way to bring yourself back into alignment and begin to reduce the energy-draining friction that contributes to burnout is restoring your connection to yourself. There's a reason phrases like "Be true to yourself," "To thine own self be true," and "Be yourself" are printed on T-shirts. There's timeless truth and wisdom hidden within the clichés.

Aligning your connection to yourself will differ for everyone but will typically include these actions:

- Un-numbing yourself, honoring your humanity, and developing compassion for the human you. Consider self-compassion and self-care: where have you been neglecting yourself?
- Putting down the mask of inauthenticity.
- Deepening your self-knowledge and getting clear on your desires.
- Front-burnering your joy by prioritizing what matters to you. Where have you betrayed yourself? Recommit yourself to your humanity and what generates energy for you.

Un-numb Yourself, Pause, and Honor Your Humanity and Pain

The first part of coming into alignment within yourself is honoring your human needs. By acknowledging your needs, you disrupt the idea that you are a machine. By slowing down, honoring your needs, and caring for yourself in the moment, you will take yourself off autopilot and begin to bring yourself into alignment.

When I use the term self-care, I do not mean bubble baths and yoga sessions, though that could be a part of your self-care plan. By self-care I literally mean caring for yourself as opposed to neglecting or outright ignoring your needs to rest, grieve, process your emotions, heal from injury, or recover from a difficult situation – or celebrate an accomplishment. Self-care causes the overworking record to skip, shifting you out of autopilot and startling you back into present awareness.

What Does This Mean?

For L'Oreal Thompson Payton, overworking on autopilot has extended beyond the workplace. It even reached to a leisurely hike with her family in her downtime. "I remember we were hiking in Hawaii last year right after Thanksgiving and I had done the hike before, no problem. But it was very different with a 20-pound toddler strapped to my back. And we were at the next-to-last summit and I could see the top and I think I would have pushed through because that's my default wiring."

But she did not push through. In that moment, she decided to honor her humanity by stopping at her limit. Maybe she'd be able to make it to the summit the following year.

And remember Jennifer from Chapter 2 – the attorney who tried to keep a Zoom appointment after learning about the death of her mentor? When I offered to reschedule our meeting in light of her loss earlier that morning, she initially declined. But once she took a moment to think it over, her machine mind switched off and her humanity stepped forward. By going in the opposite direction and reluctantly choosing to honor her humanity and fulfill her need to grieve, she took a small step toward fixing the misalignment of self-denial that can so often lead to burnout.

Whenever you are faced with the choice to ignore your emotional or physical needs and you choose yourself instead, you are doing the work to disrupt machine mindset.

Accept That You Are Worthy

For Myleik Teele, the entrepreneur we first met in Chapter 4 who, during a season of burnout, shut down a beauty subscription box business that was earning millions, overworking started out as her way to feel worthy.

"When I was hustling and a lot more ambitious, I think what I really wanted was to genuinely feel good about myself," Teele confessed. "And I thought that getting praise, making money, buying things would do that."

She did learn a lot through the sheer volume of things she accomplished during those high-energy years. But now that she's slowed her pace, she's made peace with herself and learned to find her worth outside of work.

"What I know today is that whether I show you what I do or not, the worth and value in all that I am does not go away," she said. "My goodness, my work ethic, who I am does not go away because I stop and I sit on the bench and take a breather and enjoy the view while you run back and forth. And I think that is something that I probably could not see then that I can see now. That just comes from time and experience. I am no less creative. I am no less ambitious. I'm just not turning on that burner right now."

Quiana Smith, whom we met in Chapter 4, had a similar epiphany as she recovered from her most severe season of burnout during the pandemic. Working in her organization's government practice during COVID, during a season she was up for promotion, eventually made her sick from overworking. As she healed, she realized she was pushing herself too hard.

"I focus a lot on doing and producing in order to feel as though I'm providing value when the truth is just my being is valuable," Smith said. "My presence is valuable. I do not have to produce anything."

It took her a while to accept and absorb that new mindset but once she did, she says everything changed.

Why Inauthenticity Burns You Out

Coming into alignment with yourself also requires you to accept yourself – unusual interests, quirks, and all. This is particularly difficult work because most people have been working hard to "fit in" to a wider group context since elementary school. We learn early on that being different can attract unwanted attention that puts distance between ourselves and our groups of choice. For introverts and shy personalities especially, standing out can mean standing apart, and that can be uncomfortable.

But muting yourself for the sake of blending in comes at a price. For one, denying your true self prevents you from making your unique contribution to the world. When you are not showing up as yourself, the most you can hope to show up as is a second-rate counterfeit of someone else. Living with this knowledge is soul-crushing.

Perhaps more importantly, not being yourself requires additional energy. Hiding who you are with others or code-switching – the act of changing one's language choices, mannerisms, tone of voice, or physical presentation to come across as more pleasing and acceptable – in professional settings is exhausting. And over time, that spent energy can contribute to burnout.

But authenticity – the act of simply being yourself – is generative.

Why You Do Not Know Who You Are

Similarly to the way we start trying to fit in early in life, we are also given prescribed instructions for professional success pretty early on.

Guided by well-meaning parents and teachers, we are encouraged to go to school, get good grades, graduate, and attend college for as many degrees as we can stand before entering the workforce. For the professions that present-day adults worked for years to enter, there's generally a year-by-year, step-by-step playbook with instructions on what to do when in order to make it down a particular professional path.

We first met Aundrea Cline-Thomas in Chapter 5. She was a broadcast journalist for nearly 20 years before she quit her anchor position at a local news station in New York City and opted for a career shift. Upon leaving the newsroom at age 41, she experienced the first year she had ever not had a plan for her career – and by extension her life – handed to her by someone else. It was the first time she was completely in control of where her career would go and how each day would play out.

This culturally sanctioned, engineered lack of autonomy creates a lack of self-knowledge by default, save for the intentional few who make time to regularly ponder their likes, dislikes, needs, and desires starting out in early childhood. And the lack of autonomy and self-knowledge eventually backfires.

I've seen this time and time again with coaching clients who come to me after achieving all the things – multiple degrees, numerous certifications, high-ranking positions, handsome salaries, and industry respect. Despite having it all, these high achievers sense that something is missing, yet they are at a loss as to what that something might be. As we begin to peel back the layers in our work together, I'm astonished to find that despite achieving so much, most people do not have a basic understanding of what underlying needs and desires are driving them. Without understanding their inherent drives, true fulfillment is hard to reach.

Sadly, high achievers can be simultaneously the most accomplished and yet the most exhausted members of the workforce. Because they lack self-knowledge, they waste unnecessary time and energy trying to find the path that fits. They also tend to overwork because they aren't clear on what they want to get out of their time. So they jump on the hamster wheel of overworking, assuming that more time and effort working will eventually unlock the elusive sense of fulfillment. Newsflash: it seldom if ever does.

In this way, not knowing yourself is incredibly inefficient. Getting to know yourself – what you need and what you can do without – may feel like a lot of work up front, but it is the ultimate cheat code and time hack that will help you make choices in alignment with who you are more often than not.

Honor Your Individuality

One of the clearest ways to get insight into your needs and into your identity is to take stock of what energizes you. If you are currently in the middle of burnout, you might be at a loss for what fuels you in this season. But you can reflect back as far as you need to in order to identify activities, places, and people that make you feel physically energized.

For my previous personal branding work, I have used this exercise to help my clients get clear on the kind of work they both wanted to focus on and build a narrative around for future opportunities. But truthfully, it can be used for any area of your life – including but not limited to work – to determine where you need to put more of your focus.

Looking Inward

It goes without saying that only you can ultimately determine what you really need, what generates energy for you, and who you really are. This is why, although most people receive no formal training in how to look inward for answers, direction, and guidance, you'll eventually have to stop looking outside of yourself for the answers only you have access to.

The end of machine mindset and return to humanity starts with an end of self-betrayal. An end of self-betrayal or self-denial starts within tuning in and connecting with your intuition. I want you to think of your intuition as one of your greatest assets – it's your internal mapping system, your inner GPS that will help you find your way to a more aligned path. You can deepen your connection with your intuition through stillness practices, which I'll cover more in Chapter 12, but for now understand that going inward instead of looking outside of yourself is key to taking yourself off autopilot and coming back into alignment.

Whether we are referring to your emotional need to grieve, your physical need to rest, your social need to be in community, or your recreational need to play and have fun, you honor your humanity when you tune into your needs and stop betraying yourself. Doing so reduces your vulnerability to burnout. As a bonus, front-burnering your needs and what matters to you, whether or not you understand why doing so matters, generates energy. And when you are in the midst of a burnout season, you desperately need that energy to see your way out of the exhaustion. Front-burner yourself to beat burnout.

Know Yourself

Whatever actions, people, places, or activities always make you feel your best should not be optional; they should be non-negotiable aspects of your routine.

What's your secret sauce? How is your approach different from that of everyone else? In short, what makes you *you*. If you are not sure, you are not alone. Getting clear enough to articulate what makes you unique is tough for most people. But I have found that if you examine pivotal moments – your earliest memories of feeling disappointed, torn, devastated; your first recollections of feeling powerful, exhilarated, energized; those first memories of feeling confused, furious, or that life was unfair – hidden in those deeply held memories and personal stories is magic. If you can effectively tap into those stories, you can get to the core of who you are. What do you remember? What sticks out to you, even now? How did those life events change you?

Trying to figure out the next level of your purpose? As much as you may think you need to start from zero and do something completely new, the key may be to look back at the beginning so you can see how you have always been able to summon success. Go back to the early days. Back to those foundational experiences that defined you early on. How have you always done what you do? Too many of us are reinventing the wheel thinking that finding purpose means forging ahead into the future with no regard for the past. But there's information to be found when we go back to the beginning. Reflect: what parts of your story remain unchanged through the seasons? This is the magic we are looking to uncover.

Honor Your Intuition

Just as you sometimes have a gut feeling that you should pick up a call even when you have no idea who is on the other end of the line, you have intuition that is guiding you away from things that aren't for you and toward what you should be doing with your life. On a deep level, you recognize your purpose. You fully understand exactly what you should be doing and what you are called to do. It could be the call of creative expression, or of your tribe. Maybe it's the call of freedom, or the call to give back. Or it could be the call of excellence when you know you are not giving your best effort. Whatever it means for you now may be the perfect time to answer the call and honor your intuition.

Set an intention to reconnect with your intuition. It will not only guide you back to what you want but also toward what you are meant to be doing with your gifts. When you make the choice to walk fully in your purpose, your intuition is the most valuable asset you have to lean on. The victories are always found when you tune in and trust your inner guidance and wisdom, especially when it does not make sense to you just yet.

Funny that when you look back, your biggest victories are often the ones that came after you decided to tolerate the discomfort of uncertainty, shut out the opinions of others, and tune into yourself. Honor your intuition and turn the volume up on that (still small) voice instead of begging it to be quiet. Say what you mean, and refuse to betray yourself, even if it is unpopular.

Think back to when you took a leap and said yes, even though it felt too soon, too big, too scary. When there were no guarantees. When you stopped denying what you already knew to be true. When you stopped bargaining with your future self to make do with good enough. Should you accept the offer or turn it down? Should you move forward or retreat? Should you keep offering that service or take a chance on showing up in a new way? Chances are, you already know. Think about this: if you listen to yourself, trust yourself, and honor yourself, how can that backfire? The victories are found in obedience, even when it does not make sense to you just yet.

Put Down the Mask of Inauthenticity

What if the trait that you see as a character flaw is actually your magic? What if the thing that frustrates people and ruffles their feathers about you is the thing they need the most?

So many of us spend years denying our true interests and strengths in favor of following a path directed by people whose approval we crave. It's the choice to go to law school over becoming a writer. Or to study medicine instead of becoming a business owner. And yet fulfillment is nowhere to be found because the path chosen does not align with our internal motivators.

We often avoid showing what makes us different for fear of being or doing too much. But what you are hiding could attract what's actually meant for you. What you are hiding could connect you to what you desire the most.

How can you compare yourself to someone else when you are not even showing up fully as yourself? You've probably been encouraged to stop comparing yourself to what people post about their lives on social media. But rarely are we challenged to examine whether someone else's path we may envy is the path we truly want to walk. Because most of us have yet to summon the courage to go all in for what we really want, and who we really are.

Most of us are living shadow lives, working shadow careers, chasing callings others want for us, instead of pursuing the highest expression of our own purpose. If you are not operating in the highest expression of your gift, and instead settling for a second-rate shadow version, how can you compare yourself to others who aren't even doing what you really want to do? If you feel behind, maybe you are not where you want to be because you are in a shadow arena instead of in the bright sunlight meant for you. So instead of comparing, focus and tune in to you. Decide what kind of star you really want to be, then get to work on shining so you can come out of your own shadow.

Beware of Pushback

It would be irresponsible of me not to warn you that all this new-found self-discovery will not be easy to navigate. When clarity leads to change, that change can be hard, especially if you like tradition and routine. But change can be most difficult for those around you who may have grown accustomed to a previous version of you.

Sometimes change can be hard when it's easily noticeable by the public. It's one thing to start a meditation practice in private that does not alter your routine or schedule. It's quite another to initiate a public-facing career pivot that changes your availability in the evenings or changes how much you are available to other people in general. And if your previous identity was high-profile and engendered respect and access, you have all those prying eyes to consider. What will people think? How will your changes impact their perception of you?

Let me share what I've learned from experience. When you make a big change – say, your hair color, or even your job – it may register briefly to the outside world, but after that, humans do what humans do.

They adapt.

So while you may fret endlessly about that big change you are afraid of making, once you make it, most people will barely notice. And if they do notice, the decision you lost sleep over will likely only register for a short while. The new you will become the current you, and the past you will become a memory.

So if the changes you are spending time endlessly deliberating over only register to others for a brief moment in time, there's no need to put your life on hold. There's no good reason to put off making the changes that could add more fulfillment and happiness to your days.

Is there something big you are ready to change? A relationship? A job? Where you live? Your life is not set in stone. You can change all of it, with one swift decision. The world will go on. And you will be happier for it.

What's one change that the true you is begging to make?

Key Insights

- Understanding who you are is critical when you are dealing with burnout. When you don't know what you want, you waste time and energy.
- Inauthenticity — the act of not being yourself uses a lot of energy and can also add to feelings of burnout.
- Self-care disrupts machine mindset as you begin to honor your humanity beyond the labor you produce.

10

Right-Size
Your Ambition

The second way to bring yourself back into alignment and begin to reduce the energy-draining friction that contributes to burnout is by restoring your connection to your ambition.

Right-sizing your ambition to yourself will differ for everyone, but will typically include these actions:

- Investigate and challenge your past programming.
- Recenter in your purpose.
- Right-size your goals to ensure they are a fit for where you are now.

If you have not spent a lot of time in the past clarifying what you want and what you need, it's likely that your current idea of ambition does not truly reflect your authentic career desire. Bringing your ambition into alignment means right-sizing your aspirations so they are in line with the activities and people who bring you energy, rather than those who drain you.

When you think of the Purposescaping work you did in Chapter 8, reflect on the questions that corresponded to the work of winter. When you have a moment to pause, reflect on this season of your life and make decisions about the future, what aspects of your current life need to be pruned and discarded? Which parts will you take with you into a new spring planting season?

How Ambition Misalignment Contributes to Burnout

Given that we spend roughly a third of our lives at work, the sheer number of hours spent on misaligned work alone could account for the leaked energy leading us to burnout.

After a series of close, personal loved ones passed suddenly, André Blackman, whom we met in Chapter 5, took some time with his daughter to travel and clear his head. He began reaching out to trusted colleagues to discuss what it might look like if he did something different professionally. He'd been running his boutique search firm OnBoard Health for about seven years, and in light of the success he'd achieved, the uncertainties of entrepreneurship were wearing him down.

As he reconsidered business ownership, things became clear. After a series of conversations with those in the field, Blackman received a partnership offer to do recruiting work at a larger firm. He officially joined his new organization as partner, effectively leaving the startup world. With a larger team to support his higher-level work inside an older company with more established infrastructure, he instantly had the in-house resources to do what he does best. Outside of that, he planned to rest.

Blackman said he does not regret anything and he definitely does not feel like a failure for shuttering his business. In his opinion, his business gave him a platform to be noticed and provided the pathway to partner.

In the process of winding down OnBoard Health – redirecting prospects to his new full-time gig and letting go of the team members who previously supported him – he had a chance to reflect on what he was able to accomplish.

"There's something about being recognized for how I showed up in this industry," he said. "There's a pathway I created for myself.

Pulse and Signal was the blog that turned into writing and speaking. Then that turned into a company – the strategy consultancy where I was able to work with digital health startups."

Sometimes ambition alignment will require a pivot. Blackman encourages others to use their body of work to transition to the next level. As a recruiter, he says he's seen other people – particularly highly accomplished Black women – have a chance to make a similar pivot but undersell themselves because of self-doubt or the desire to be of service.

And when professionals are passionate about their work – especially mission-driven work – they can set themselves up to be undercompensated. "You're like, oh I'm just here to help," he said. "We're not doing that. Because people can sense that and [take advantage]. This is not your Mother Theresa moment."

But it's a message he first had to share with himself. As he pivoted his ambition away from entrepreneurship, he got clear that he wanted to be of service, but he had no desire to burn himself out trying to be helpful. "Stop this whole martyrdom; it's not helping anybody."

Blackman's story is a great illustration of what happens when a career season has come and gone. While entrepreneurship fit his ambitions for a clear period of his life and may one day fit again, once that season was over, the misalignment he felt made it difficult to continue without a pivot.

Getting Clear

If, like Blackman, your ambition feels misaligned, the first part of bringing your ambition into alignment is to get clear on what your current ambition is. In my previous book, *Package Your Genius: 5 Steps to Build Your Most Powerful Personal Brand,* I went into detail about how one can clarify and amplify a message around the work they want to do in this season.

I won't go into full detail here, but the Package Your Genius process is important when you need that critical clarity for your next phase. The steps are as follows:

1. **Get clear on your brand.** Find clarity by reconnecting with your childhood self, identifying your strengths and skills, and communicating your genius in a concise message.
2. **Make the case.** Use case studies to tell the story of your career and back-up your newly articulated message by showing evidence of your past performance, work, and value. Secure social proof from colleagues, mentors, and others who can vouch for your skills.
3. **Define your big ideas.** Uncover your thought leadership message and create content that gets that message into the world. Extend your content to brand signatures that allow you to monetize and further brand your expertise.
4. **Make yourself visible.** Tap into social media and digital tools to build an online presence, and when you are ready, share your ideas though public speaking and with the media. Continuously grow and nurture your network.
5. **Sell yourself.** Be proactive and intentionally go after opportunities. Master your time and train yourself to be productive.

When it comes to aligning your ambition, step one of the Package Your Genius process is key.

Clarify Your Genius

The Package Your Genius process offers you a way to get back in tune with your own judgment, just as you did as a child.

What does this have to do with your personal brand? Well, if you are in touch with yourself and who you really are, you'll be able to get that much closer to the real purpose and assignment for your life. You'll then be able to clearly communicate that to the people it can serve. Instead of trying to fit yourself into a box, when you package your genius, you unleash your magic. And I assure you, nothing feels better than that.

Set an intention to reconnect with your intuition because it will guide you not only back to what you want but also toward what you are meant to be doing with your gifts. Here's an overview of the questions you want to ask:

- Who are you?
- What are your strengths?
- What problems do you solve?
- Who is your audience?
- What is your mode of working?

Let's dive into the questions.

The Big Question: Who Are You?

How do you know who you are? One proven way to answer the question is to first identify your strengths. I'm not going to turn this into a book on strengths because there are dozens of wonderful books on that topic, but I will share an overview of how to figure out your strengths, as well as a few tools that will help you.

Why strengths? I firmly believe that your strengths are your *truth mirrors*; they reflect your authenticity back to you. Strengths are like the cardinal directions of your internal compass. If it's grown too quiet and you cannot quite hear your internal voice anymore, your strengths are fantastic guideposts.

So how do we find our strengths? There are internal and external clues.

Internal Clues to Your Strengths

First, let's talk about the internal clues. What brings you alive? What energizes you? What do you look forward to doing? When do you feel a sense of flow?

(continued)

(*continued*)

Practically speaking, you can look at what Michael Bungay Stanier described in his book *Do More Great Work* as "peak moments." Essentially, you want to look back over your working life and begin cataloging those moments when you felt physically energized by your work.

Marcus Buckingham talks about a similar sensation in his book *Go Put Your Strengths to Work*. Buckingham asks readers to make a list of things they loved and things they loathed. Not surprisingly, when it comes to your working life, those "loved it" moments are a clue to your most natural strengths.

Take a minute to jot down a few of the peak moments that you have experienced in your career. If you are hard-pressed to think of any career peak moments, think back to a time when you were doing purposeful work, either in the community, your church, with your family, or even in school. You'll be referencing those later.

Another way to get closer to your strengths is to zero in on the parts of your work that drain you. The problem with focusing solely on your strengths is that you can make the mistake of solving the right problem for the wrong audience, approaching the right audience with the wrong solution, or delivering the right solution in the wrong format.

Basically, if you only focus on your strengths you may end up with work that takes you almost to the fulfillment line but stops short and feels incomplete.

Take a second to think about what *drains* you. Think about your current tasks, colleagues, or clients. There may be aspects of the work you enjoy even though other parts drain you. These are things you'll want to automate, delegate, or avoid altogether.

What drains you about your work?

Finding Your Strengths Externally

After you spend some time doing the self-reflection that only you can do to identify the internal clues of your strengths, then it's time to look at your external clues. The external clues can be found by asking yourself another series of questions.

First, what do people thank you for? This is one of my very favorite questions to ask because most people do not think about it at all. Far too many of us are oblivious to the gratitude we receive from others, yet gratitude is a tremendous indicator of where others are receiving value from us. I'm of the opinion that you cannot plan to grow your audience or expect people to promote you or pay for your services if you do not first add value to their lives.

Next question: what do people always ask for your help with? This is the opposite side of the gratitude question. If you have a hard time remembering the last time you received gratitude (or maybe the people in your life are largely ungrateful, which is another problem altogether), think instead about what people ask for your help with. For many people, that's a much easier question to tackle. The great thing about this question is that it typically shows up in every area of your life, if you think broadly enough.

For example, as a coach I am typically responsible for helping people activate something new in their lives. That could mean launching a new brand podcast, igniting a business, or getting started with a new book project. Not so ironically, I'm also tasked with "getting the ball rolling" at home. Whenever it's time to move a big project forward, I'm typically the person those in my family or circle of friends turn to. In that way, I'm

(continued)

(continued)

asked to help activate new ideas and am thanked for being the catalyst for major changes.

Where do you receive consistent gratitude across all areas of your life? What contribution do people consistently thank you for?

Look at What's Working

You now know how to go about examining the internal and external clues to your strengths. But there are more ways to examine the direction your personal brand should take.

Look at your life – what's working? What is really working well? Reflect back on the past year, or for those of you who have been in your field for a while, the total length of your career. Reflect on your professional roles and community involvement. What's working well for you at work?

When you can identify your strengths, what energizes you and what the world is already mirroring back to you in the form of gratitude, clarity is inevitable for both you and the audience with whom you plan to connect.

The American Dream Is Changing

If, after spending time with the Purposescaping process, you feel your priorities have shifted significantly, you are not alone.

After the pandemic, Todd Rose and his think tank team at Populace published several indices using private opinion methodologies to better understand what workers truly prioritize. When asked to compare their job priorities before the pandemic to now, their American Workforce Index showed that two-thirds of workers said their priorities had shifted at least a bit, with almost one in five saying their priorities had changed a lot. Only 27% said their job priorities were the same as before the pandemic.

One of the major permanent changes is the desire for more workplace flexibility. Workers now rank the ability to work remotely as their second highest priority, and having time for other important things in life while working as their fourth highest priority.

The Populace Success Index explored how Americans personally define success and the American Dream. It identified two powerful ideas – success is about a meaningful life, not about getting rich, and the American Dream is personal, not financial.

According to their research, half of Americans' top 10 priorities for success focus on a meaningful life. These include doing work that positively impacts others, enjoying their work, being pleasant to be around, having a purpose, and being actively involved in their community. In contrast, being rich is ranked near the bottom (45 out of 61).

The Success Index also revealed that most Americans believe that the American Dream is about personal success – achieving what matters most to you. Yet they think that most others define it in purely economic terms, as the ability to achieve financial prosperity through hard work.

The Role of Purpose

I've been coaching high-performing professionals including C-Suite leaders for more than a decade – all of them extremely skilled and talented at what they do. However, instead of leaning into ease, most of the high achievers I've coached fall into extreme overworking. They achieve great things of course, but they end up completely depleted at some point in the journey.

At a certain point, they realize the way they're working is no longer working for them and for them to achieve a greater sense of fulfillment they'll have to finally begin prioritizing their needs as human beings. They'll have to start leaning more into work that brings them joy, and is aligned to their greater life purpose.

During our work together, I ask my clients to reflect deeply on their career journeys. I want them to get clear on what work, work arrangements, teams, and workplace cultures have left them feeling more energized than depleted. Believe it or not, most people don't naturally consider what makes one work environment work better for them than another. We're taught to consider job compensation, benefits, and the prestige of a company to determine whether a job is a good fit. But even if a person is hitting benchmarks and achieving unprecedented success – which is generally the case for most high achievers – without a sense of connection to their purpose and an alignment between the work environment and the person's individual needs – they will typically feel as though something is missing.

How to Clarify Your Current Desires and Hungers

Only you know what drives you. Only you have the answer about what work is the most purposeful for you. Callings call.

Why does it even matter whether or not you align your work with your purpose? Who cares if you explore what you are meant to do? What difference does it make if you do not share your genius with others?

Those are the questions I want us to explore now. Because before I can make the case that you should align your ambition closer to your purpose, you should first understand what's at stake if you do not.

I believe the mandate of being human – what's written in our genetic code or whatever makes us Homo sapiens versus some other species – is to find what we were put on this earth to do. Your mandate as a human is to fulfill the assignment and complete the mission for your specific journey, your specific life. That is what I wholeheartedly believe.

But if we are honest with ourselves, our life missions have likely been evident since childhood or adolescence. We've heard the call. But how many of us answered and chose to walk down the path our calling was leading us to?

I can remember being a student in middle school and then again in high school. I loved my English classes. My classmates and teachers were all convinced that one day I'd be a famous, important writer whose words would touch millions of people.

Somewhere along the way, I bought into the idea of "the starving artist" and decided I could not be a successful writer without starving first. So while I always knew that I was sent here to write, for years I did not do it.

Despite my successes as a PR person and a coach, until I finally sat down and wrote my first book, I did not feel at home in my success. There was always this lingering static; I can't quite describe it, but it was like a cloud hanging over me. And it was as if the cloud was saying, "I mean, this is nice and everything, but when are you going to write your book?" As if nothing else I'd done mattered for real.

And then once I got that book out there, just like that, the dissonance cleared. The cloud passed.

Now, I will be honest. The dissonance came back. But when it did, I was crystal clear on why. I know I have more books to write, and this book is proof of that. I know I have more messages to leave this planet while I still have an earthly vessel that can help me accomplish what I'm here to do in this realm.

Callings call. So expect it to feel a little uncomfortable when you are not picking up the phone.

It's like that feeling that you forgot to do something important, but you cannot quite put your finger on what that something is. Or when you make out your list for the store, and you go shopping, but you know there's something you forgot; even though you got every single thing on the list, something still seems to be missing.

And answering the call is the opposite. Instead, it's the feeling of a stocked pantry, or of all the bills being paid, or all the doctor's appointments scheduled – the feeling that nothing is falling through the cracks.

But when you willingly deny yourself the opportunity to answer the call or, to use my term, "package your genius," you create an internal sense of restlessness that haunts you. And that restlessness will continue to haunt you until you honor – in some way – what you were put here to do.

Until you pick up that metaphorical call, you may not be able to put your finger on it, but you'll always get the sense that *something* is missing.

How to Update Your Goals and Plans According to Your Current Hungers

L'Oreal Thompson Payton was climbing the ladder at a major magazine – on her way to the editor-in-chief position she'd dreamed about since childhood. But she felt like the goal post kept moving and the metrics against which her performance was judged just kept going up. With a new baby and a book in progress, the demands of climbing the ladder in her nine-to-five became too much.

Her performance review noted that she had exceeded her goals for page views – the key metric of her performance – but was only meeting expectations in her role as a writer. She felt like no matter how hard she worked, it was never sufficient.

"I can give my all, go above and beyond, and it's never going to be enough," Payton said. After experiencing this particular phenomenon of meeting a target only to have the target move, Payton decided she'd had enough. She chose herself, her peace, and her mental health and got off the hamster wheel. "I no longer am subscribing to that," Payton declared. "I'm gonna choose a different way."

She left the newsroom for freelance writing, and picked up her yoga teaching certification on the side. While she doesn't know if freelance is forever, right now it's the best scenario for her nervous system. "Everything is coming into alignment, where I feel like before I was trying to fit myself into a box that perhaps was never really meant for me in the first place," she said.

Payton originally believed she had to work up to a senior writer position, and to become an award-winning journalist, she needed to work at one of the best newsrooms in the country. That you have to have lots of accolades and bylines. "There was certainly a part of me that bought in to that – I had dreams of becoming editor in chief of a teen magazine since I was literally a teen myself," she said.

But when her literary heroine Toni Morrison died, Payton had a moment. "I think that was the first time I was like, oh, it's 'enough' [to be a writer]. It's always been enough. I just never accepted it as enough to be a writer because in our industry, you want to be the editor, you want to be the one making the shots, you want to get paid more money. And that seemed to be the track that guaranteed those things and that success."

Aligning Your Ambition to Purposeful Work Is Energizing

Although it would seem that the solution to work-fueled exhaustion and burnout is extended rest, many professionals find themselves energized once they have aligned their daily working lives to the work that feels more purposeful to them. That's because aligning your ambition to your purpose – instead of prestige or an arbitrary monetary number – generates energy.

Payton says she's always felt like she was on a quest for meaning and fulfillment in her career, and finally some 15 years into her journey, she's found it. And she only found it when she stopped trying to fit into a box of misaligned career ambition.

"I'm bigger than the box," Payton told me. "I do not have to be on the masthead, I do not have to be the one in charge. I want to write meaningful stories that impact people. And that's what I'm able to do now and do freely because I jumped out of the box."

She had to trust that she was enough and that her gifts, talents, and writing would be enough to carry her. So far that's been the case. "Shortly after I left [my full-time job], all of these doors started to open. Like I talked about I want to write a column and that's in the works. I want to write a cover story and that's going to come out. I think everything happens when it's supposed to."

She's still working hard – arguably harder than before – to meet her new career ambitions. But luckily for her, having had the work-twice-as-hard mentality means that Payton feels prepared for whatever lies ahead. "I have prepared for this moment for 15-plus career years, going back further into high school and in college, writing on the student newspapers. And also I have done the work and I have prepared to meet the moment. And now that I'm like, hey, I'm ready and I'm open, the opportunities are coming. I think that manifestation is doing the work and meeting the moment. When that intersects, then it's like, oh, now all these things that I have dreamed about are coming to fruition."

But she acknowledges that it requires a leap of faith that many professionals are conditioned not to take because of the risk. "It's not stable; it's scary," Payton said. "Good girls like me aren't supposed to quit their day jobs and become entrepreneurs and freelance writers especially. There's a lot of risk in the art."

Now that she's made the switch and right-sized her ambition, Payton says her nervous system is in the process of recalibrating. She's feeling at ease as she emerges from burnout, and she feels happier and more fulfilled. "I was with a mentor the other day and she was like, you are literally glowing."

How to Pivot Your Ambition If Necessary

If your situation is straightforward like Payton's, take her lead and right-size your career ambitions by revising your level of work. That may look like downshifting from management back to an individual contributor. Or on the converse, it may look like accepting that you are ready for leadership and yearn to lead a team. If you want to remain active in your current industry and even your current organization but want to change your level of seniority, get clear on whether you want to move up, down, or lateral before broaching that conversation with your leader.

But if your situation is not as straightforward and burnout has made you realize that you need to pivot into a completely new industry or type of role, here's how to make your move.

Explore Your Career Misalignment to Uncover Your Current Career Passion

If you are employed, what's not working in your current role? What's missing in the work you are doing now? Think about how you'd be most energized spending your time. Look to your volunteer work, extracurricular activities, and hobbies for clues on what might bring you professional passion.

Get Clear on Your Values

Reflect on your values for this season of your life and determine what your priorities are for your next role. Potential values include compensation levels, location of the role, total benefits package, workplace flexibility, your ability to work remotely, your direct access to leadership, hands-on experience, the community impact of your work, your ability to travel, and more.

Match Your Passions and Values to a Professional Pivot

If the new type of work you are interested in is a clear departure from the work you have been known for, you may have to do a little research to find professional work that lines up with the new vision you have for your career. Make a list of the actionable skills you'd like to use in your new career identity. What types of jobs come to mind? If nothing pops up, plug a few of your ideal skills into LinkedIn jobs to see what types of roles pop up. What stands out from that list?

Make a list of ideal titles and industries to help you fine-tune the information you gathered on potential roles. Decide on the industry and specific title that speaks to you the most. Cross-check this with your values. For example, if flexibility and work-life balance matter more to you than compensation, a pressure cooker field like commercial banking may not be the best fit. Alternatively, if compensation and ability to travel are your top values, a career in nonprofits may not hold your commitment for very long. Be honest with yourself about what you value and the order those values rank in priority.

Craft a Narrative That Bridges Your Skills

If you are making a career pivot, it will be important to highlight the transferable skills you are bringing from your previous role. But you may also find that the work you are seeking falls under a broader umbrella category of the type of opportunities you have sought out your whole life.

For example, in my thought leadership and personal brand coaching work, I found that one of the most powerful skills I have to help clients is the skill of storytelling. I gained storytelling skills in both my work as a journalist and as a creative writer. I always had the desire to shed light on the stories of people and groups I thought more folks should know about. While I did this as a journalist in the community, the desire to shed light on worthy stories was the same desire that drives my personal brand and thought leadership coaching work where I help people make their talents stand out.

Try to find the underlying desire driving everything you have done so you can better communicate why you are the best at the new work you want to do.

Audit Your Network and Connect

One beauty of having a career built on pivots is the cumulative network you have gathered on the journey. If you have pivoted your skills in the past, you have likely had to get to know new groups of people, join new professional associations, and network at new organizations along the way. Now's the time to tap back into this network you have amassed. Armed with your bridge narrative, set a goal to reconnect with two to three people each week to have a conversation (by email, virtually, or in person). During the conversation, let your colleague know what you are up to now, what you are curious about, and how they can be on the lookout for opportunities that may be aligned with your current goals.

They will likely be able to help you continue brainstorming target organizations that could be a good new professional home for you on the other end of your pivot. If you have come to an impasse in your pivot, stay encouraged. The more you brainstorm, the more aligned your vision will become. The more people you share your new career vision with, the higher the chances someone will come across an aligned opportunity and think of you.

Key Insights

- There is no point in striving to achieve someone else's ambition, yet most people are in pursuit of a dream that does not belong to them.
- When you are out of alignment with your ambition, you may end up doing a lot of meaningful things that mean nothing to you.
- Only you know what drives you. Only you have the answer about what work is the most purposeful for you.
- Callings call and will make your misalignment uncomfortable until you give attention to what's not working, or the ambition you have not given yourself permission to pursue.
- Ambition alignment – finding the purposeful work that matters to you – creates energy.

11

Align Your Time

The third way to bring yourself back into alignment and begin to reduce the energy-draining friction that contributes to burnout is by reclaiming your time. This action will differ for everyone, but will typically include these actions:

- Increase your personal efficiency.
- Set better boundaries.
- Prioritize your energy.
- Prioritize rest by taking the time you've earned.

Coming home to yourself and honoring your human needs necessitates that you align your time with what matters to you through a mix of boundaries, personalization, energy prioritization, and personal efficiency. *What are you not making time for?*

Personal Efficiency

First things first. You likely have a lot of wasted time due to inefficiency. Now before you get wound up, please know I am not blaming your burnout on your lack of productivity. But chances are you're wasting some of your time and allowing others to waste it too because you don't have an intentional grasp on what you want to use your time on.

Thus, one of the first steps in realigning your time is to get clear on where you are the drama. This is important because I'm going to ask you to set boundaries and push back on others' demands. I'm also going to ask you to begin integrating some new practices into your life to help you feel better. All of that will require more time, so we need to create some margin in your schedule before we attempt to add anything else to your plate.

Get Organized and Use a Planning System

It's much harder to keep tabs on your time if you don't have a clear system to track where you're spending your hours. Don't take these recommendations as a personal assault – there are likely people who are taking advantage of your time. But if you're disorganized and unaware of where your time is going, you're working inefficiently by default. Without organization it will be harder to see where you have room to tighten up or where you have redundancies in your schedule that you can push back on.

By getting organized, you'll be able to make the case for why certain meetings are unnecessary, if your involvement is redundant, and whether your time could be better spent elsewhere. Even if you don't make a habit of wasting your own time, when people think you're available to lighten their loads, they'll end up wasting it. So take control of your days by planning your weeks. I'll repeat that. Take control of your days by planning your weeks in advance. Take control of your weeks by planning your months in advance. Take control of your months by looking at your year to see what's on the horizon and how you can start preparing now for what's ahead.

Remember, if you don't have a plan for your time, others will fill your time up.

I'm not a stickler for a specific type of system. I personally have found great success with the Full Focus planning system by Michael Hyatt that breaks down planning with a quarterly approach. For some people that's too much; they like a simpler planner. But I've found it works well for me and I use that with my online calendar to keep track of scheduling for my appointments, home maintenance, children's school, and clients. The planner works to give me a daily overview of what I have to do as a part of my family and business organization. The calendar helps me collaborate with others who need visibility to our shared time.

I've also used project management systems in the past and find they work well when collaborating with teams. But on the most basic level, I recommend everyone have either a paper or electronic record of their upcoming tasks, appointments, travel commitments, and to-dos. There are too many options available to rely on your memory and risk having details fall through the cracks.

Time Batching and Theming

When my sons were very young and my business was as well, people would often ask me how I got so much done. In addition to coaching, consulting, and speaking, I am also a mom of two school-aged boys, who were babies when I started my business. Back then, I didn't have the resources to hire a ton of additional support so I had to get very efficient with how I used my time in order to show up the way I wanted as a mom and uphold my high standards for the service I delivered to clients.

Compartmentalizing my time and upholding clear boundaries were habits I picked up when my children were very young and I was growing my business while working from home. I realized very early on that if I only had an hour to be productive, I was better off focusing on one task that I could do repetitively in volume.

Instead of returning one client call, posting one marketing message on social media, and drafting half of a blog post, I found that if I focused that hour on a single task – say, writing and scheduling 30 social media updates for the next few days – my work product would be much better and I would actually be able to cross something pretty substantial off my to-do list.

One of the tools to career clarity is the use of talent assessments to give you a baseline description of your workplace strengths. From the CliftonStrengths talent assessment of 34 key strengths (formerly known as Strengthsfinder), my top strength is Achiever, which means I thrive on a sense of things getting done, and feeling like I've been able to cross something off of my list. So for me, accomplishing tasks in batches instantly allows me to move the needle instead of feeling like I'm running from task to task but not making a dent in any one area.

Batching tasks – taking one type of task and doing it in volume – helped me get my schedule back. *Theming,* on the other hand, is the act of taking several task batches that fall within the same category (let's say content creation) and scheduling all of those batches on the same day of the week. Theming revolutionized my scheduling process in many ways but especially when it came to making appointments. It gave me parameters so I could set boundaries. For instance, if someone asked if I was available to meet for coffee on a Tuesday (my content day), unless that coffee was going to give me content ideas or included an interview for my podcast, I politely declined.

Along the same lines, I found that I was more effective if I scheduled my coaching calls or administrative work or creative thinking on one themed day because it allowed me to get in the zone and stay focused.

The science supports batching and theming. Neuroscientists have reported that constantly switching between different types of tasks wears on your cognitive resources and has the added drawback of making you feel tired more quickly than if you focused on one thing. This seemingly small shift allowed me to stay in control of my schedule and helped me to gauge when I did or didn't have time to take on new things or meet with people.

I have used batching and theming to hack my schedule and improve my productivity especially when time has been scarce. Batching and theming are perfect if you have a demanding schedule but still want to make time for your own goals, projects, or self-care. When you have limited spare time, you have to work to maximize the time that you do have so you can make it work for you.

Batching and theming are also great for anyone who is in a new role, responsible for leading a new team, a new parent, or has launched a new business. Basically, if you're staring at your computer screen – or into the eyes of your new baby – and you need to figure out how you'll organize your time in light of these changes, batching and theming can help you bring more structure to your days.

If you're like many of my clients who are leaving corporate America, you are used to having your schedule dictated by your boss or colleagues. But when your schedule is up to you, how will you manage your time?

Boundaries

We've all fallen victim to others' propensity to waste our time. While we can't necessarily control what people do, we can train them on how to better treat us with the boundaries we set. If you're not in a position of power, you may not think you have the right or influence to set boundaries with those who hold more power than you. But there's a way to do it subtly where you're not making demands or being a princess; you're just being a reasonable human being.

Setting boundaries with those around you may require some upfront work on your part to establish the new pace of the relationship. But trust me, it will be well worth it once your preferences become the new standard operating procedures. Following are a few simple ways to set boundaries with others.

Insist on a Meeting Agenda

How many meetings have you attended that felt completely unnecessary, went nowhere, and wasted everyone's time? That's generally due to poor leadership but can be solved with a fairly simple meeting agenda that, according to Michael Hyatt, addresses the four Ds:

- Direction: What is this meeting going to help us accomplish?
- Deliverables: What are the tasks that need to get done next?
- Doers: Who owns each task?
- Deadline: What date will these tasks be due?

Take Back Control of Your Calendar from Others

Take better ownership of your time so you become less reactive and more proactive – so you're able to carve out more time to think.

First, take some time to review your current calendar, as I covered earlier. Take inventory of recurring meetings and assess whether they require your participation. Would that time be better spent elsewhere?

Next, if you have the authority, remove yourself from unnecessary recurring meetings. If you don't have the authority, uncover what would make better use of your time. Based on the four Ds, how could you make a bigger difference with your time moving one of those meetings meaningfully forward instead of attending it? Get clear on this first so you can make the case to your boss. Try to show how *not* attending the meeting will help you turn in a better deliverable on a faster schedule.

Block Thinking Time on Your Calendar

If you're leading a team of any size, you need to build in executive thinking time to devote to considering the decisions that will better guide your team. Good decisions don't just happen. Strategic moves don't appear out of thin air – they require research, consideration, and the weighing of options. In short, good decisions and solid strategies require you to have ample thinking time on a regular basis.

Depending on your seniority, you may or may not have the authority to block time in the middle of the day, for example. But that's all the more reason why you must become more efficient with the time you do have control over, because you'll need to add thinking time into your mix.

If you can't carve out at least 30 minutes during the workday, try to carve it out in the morning before the day begins.

Decide What You Are – and Are Not – Available For

Sometimes when you have great relationships with colleagues, you'll end up having to set limits and boundaries with them because you can't be available to talk about or support them with everything.

In this case, you'll have to decide what you're available for and what you're *not* available for.

One of my clients was roughly one year into a new, very senior role where she had leadership over many colleagues she'd worked with for over a decade. These colleagues were more than co-workers; many had become friends. Due to the personal nature of her relationship with so many of the people who now reported up to someone who reported to her, her desk became the default stop whenever anyone had a grievance with their boss, a question about their workload, or a concern about compensation. She found that her day became so overrun with a flood of these tiny personnel conversations she wasn't able to move the needle on the bigger responsibilities of her role.

It was difficult because she cared deeply for her colleagues, but they were taking advantage of her affection and eating up undue amounts of her time. I had her sit down and decide what she was accessible for and what she wasn't available for. She decided that while she loved her colleagues as individuals and friends, she couldn't do their boss's jobs by entertaining the personnel issues that were, frankly, below her paygrade. She began to redirect folks to their direct managers.

When it came to interpersonal peer-to-peer issues, she was no longer available. If people had problems that they'd not yet discussed with their direct manager, she began to advise them to tell the person they report to *first*. She came to see that if an issue didn't warrant a conversation with their manager, it definitely didn't warrant a conversation with her.

She was also no longer available to get in the weeds on each individual's job roles and responsibilities, specific assignments, and specific tasks. In many cases she lacked the complete perspective to be helpful. She began to tell people, again, to go to their direct manager/ department head to have conversations about compensation or retention, or to work on solving issues within a single department. The department head should be the first call.

She also looked at her work and asked herself what she was available to be accessible for. She decided she wanted to lean in more on mentoring and strategic advice about navigating the workplace and/or her colleagues' bigger career goals, supporting the great work of the industry, solving interdepartmental issues, and addressing bigger strategic issues facing the company.

Ramp Up Your Efficiency and Organization to Balance Cutbacks

Set aside an hour block at the end of the week to "close the loop" on outstanding items and conversations from the week. You may use this hour to send invites, circle back on requests, revisit open conversations, and tie up loose ends before the weekend.

Personalization

Create a Vision with the Ideal Day Exercise

A few years ago I worked with Jamie Jensen, a storytelling consultant, to help me create a new vision for my writing career. I was coaching, speaking, and running groups full-time but I wanted to understand how to fit writing articles, essays, and into my working life.

She gave me a powerful exercise that forced me to imagine what I wanted. I've referred back to my responses to that exercise and been astonished with how closely my current reality mirrors the answers I took the time to reflect on in response to her prompts.

This is the exercise:

- Share your ideal day with me.
- Share your ideal week with me.
- Now share your ideal month with me.
- Share your ideal year with me.

When you do this exercise, fully reflect on and answer a question before moving ahead to the next one. I found this exercise so powerful because it forced me to embrace what I really wanted and how I really wanted to spend my time. It also forced me to evaluate how far away I was from my ideal day, week, month, and year.

When you decide on an ideal day, you're putting a stake in the sand. Once you've articulated what an ideal day looks like, you're forced to make decisions about your ideal week that will facilitate delivery of more ideal days than not, and so on and so forth. If you are at a loss for what you want to do, or how you want your career to go, thinking too big can be a trap. But starting with just one ideal day is a manageable way to tune into what you want out of your time.

Design an Annual Schedule for This Life Season

Ronnie Dickerson Stewart is an executive coach who spent nearly two decades charting an award-winning career in advertising, media, and tech. She made her way to the C-suite in corporate America before pivoting to a bridge role, then making a full exit while pregnant with her third child. She launched her coaching company OhHeyCoach in 2016 and now works with leaders and organizations across the inter-section of the advertising, media, marketing, PR, brand, and tech indus-tries. She works to equip leaders with new considerations, tools, and provocative guidance to aid them in designing a career and life on *their terms* rather than the terms handed to them.

"What I've learned over the decades of work is that there is an extent to which you can do a lot of things, but you can't do every-thing," Stewart told me. "And you can often end up really frustrated trying to do all the things at the same rate, at the same level of energy."

Growing up, she was inspired by watching her mother design a work cadence and schedule that worked for their family. Her mother worked in a high-risk role, but took the month of December off every year and then retired early. "I always remember around December, she wasn't working. She was fully engaged in being a parent and doing all the things that allowed us to really be in the season," Stewart remembers.

While December encompassed the busy holiday season, Stewart said her mother's annual break sent a clear message: there's a season for rest, and you can design your work and your life in a way that considers your needs. "For her, it looked like, I'm going to do overtime in the other seasons so that I can be restful in this season."

Stewart says she's been historically stretched in Q4 because in her industry Q4 is a big deal for everyone. "You're racing through Q4 to hit specific goals, and then you're racing to the beginning of the year to set new ones or to examine how you've delivered and sometimes your actual livelihood, your client relationships, and so on are based on that level of intention and vigor in that time period," Stewart said. "And there's nothing wrong with that. I just know that for me, in this season, it's not for me."

Stewart built her coaching company so that her client contracts and commitments were orchestrated in a way that allowed her to have clear downtime. "I'm not doing client engagements in Q4," she said. "I have a few, but it's not me at 100%. It's me more like 30% of that or maybe even 20% of the activation side of work."

Instead, she spends Q4 to build relationships, nurture new ones, and show gratitude and appreciation. She is deliberate about spending time in real life with clients, and has embraced that part of the year as a natural time of connection both with family and with business.

Over the past couple of years, her new schedule has been put to the test. One year after she had recently given birth, she scaled things back seasonally to see if calibrating her tempo through the year could be a sustainable approach to the work.

"As I was trying to figure out how I want to set up my work and how I wanted to serve this year, I made some very specific decisions in terms of how I want to test how I use my time," she said. That looked like designing contracts and client relationships that got lighter by Q4 and heavier at other points in the year, so that even financially, the cash flow and business operations side were still supported.

After seeing how taking time off in Q4 worked so well, Stewart decided to try taking summers slower to account for life at home with three school-aged children. She wanted to be present for the end-of-school-year hustle, and to ensure everyone in her house was on the same page for summer travel.

But while Stewart had planned on taking a slow summer approach, she was forced to realign her own strategies again when her brother unexpectedly passed away. So in the midst of her grief, she had to examine how she wanted to work, how much she was available to work, and how she could get the support of others in her business.

"You never get on the other side of grief. It's just something that's a part of your life. But now in this season of coming out of that, I now know it's possible to have a lower hum in the summer months when my kids are home as well as the winter months," she said.

Armed with proof that downshifting and upshifting can work, she says she is aiming for seven months of high activity and five months of lower activity each year. She also talks to her corporate clients about how they can apply that same thinking to their roles to the extent that they have agency over their time. "A lot of the folks who I work with are pretty seasoned executives, so they have a lot of positions of power and they have time agency," Stewart said. "They don't always see it."

She helps her clients reset and remix their time to fit the realities of their lives, and she says this is possible for most employees. It may look like working at a slower pace during certain seasons, or taking on different points of client work. In one season you may delegate more heavily. In another season you may naturally want to be more active. In one season you may pull back.

"You're still putting points on the board, but you could actually design your leadership seat in a way that feels a lot like what I have, where there are different hums and seasons where you're expressing your magic, talents, and gifts," she said. "But also you're not completely eroding yourself in the course of work because you didn't have a time to calibrate to what your bigger needs are with your lifestyle."

While Stewart was intentionally beginning the process of redesigning her approach to work and time, life does what it does, forcing her to maneuver around her grief. Most people haven't taken that intentional time to design how best to account for life's unexpected circumstances. But when they do, they'd likely find that their just-in-case plan works better across the board, crisis or not.

Stewart recommends that employees examine the seasonal aspects of their industries and get clear on the busy seasons, when leaders are engaged, when certain types of work are being prioritized, and when budgets are moving or being examined. When are the lulls? When do things naturally slow down? How can you build your work around that? "I've learned that from coming up in the industry. So what I've done is started to marry my activity to not exactly match the seasonality of advertising, but to be responsive to it."

Energy Prioritization

Your time, while influenced by other factors and powers, is still your time. You get a say in how the hours that comprise your life are spent. Once you've trimmed the fat through efficiency, give some of that time back to yourself by investing it in the activities and relationships that refuel you. Invest that time back into your EGAs (energy-generating activities) and EGRs (energy-generating relationships).

Prioritize Your Energy-Generating Activities (EGAs)

We've talked about the work that brings you energy, and I'll share more about the people who bring your energy (your EGRs) in Chapter 13. If we agree that purposeful work and hobbies are energizing, if we agree that certain people in our lives are energizing, and we also agree that we are running at an energy deficit during burnout, it stands to reason that we need to prioritize the things and people that can put more fuel in our energy tank.

This is a mindset shift you'll have to make for yourself if you want to break the cycle of running on empty. Remember, machine mindset doesn't consider your humanity because machines don't need energy to operate. But you're not a machine; you're a biological and spiritual being in need of a specific set of nutrients to perform at your best. Whatever those nutrients are for you – refer back to Chapter 8 and the work you did on Purposescaping – make a decision to prioritize them because they are the key to your restoration.

Put Your Priorities on the Calendar

The same way you need to safeguard how much access others have to your calendar, you need to be proactive about putting the things that matter to you on your calendar in advance if you want to ensure they happen.

This is an extension of your energy-generating activities, work, and relationships. Since you need the energy to get out of burnout, make sure you're making room and time for the things that energize you!

Plan in advance for the things that energize you. That may mean planning a quarterly gathering of your industry colleagues if your professional community is something that matters to you but you're not getting enough of it. That may mean signing up and paying for a weekly yoga class if you find that keeps you calibrated. Stop treating the things that help you show up as your best as optional indulgences. They're what you need to put on the front burner if you want to end chronic burnout and find your way back to balance.

Whenever possible, you should make deposits in yourself at the beginning of your day. Invest in the practices that generate energy before you give yourself to the tasks that may deplete you.

In fact, several people who experienced the cycle of burnout I described earlier in the book mentioned that after a burnout breaking point, their first recalibration was their morning routine. They got clear on what they needed early in the day to be their very best, and then designed their workday to accommodate that unique need. Some took it as far as to not take meetings in the morning so they could enjoy time in nature or have solitude for prayer. Others took time for a purpose-filled passion project before seeing patients in the afternoon. You may not have the autonomy to start your workday at noon, but if you get clear on what you need to be your best self and make a plan to front-load your day with even 30 minutes of that, I believe you'll experience a powerful shift.

When you start your morning with what you need to be centered and tackle your to-do list only once you have tended to yourself, you will likely be more productive when you design your time in a way that centers your needs.

Identify and Prioritize EGAs That Restore Personal Goals

Let's get a little introspective and use your emotions to guide you to your EGs. Think about what's missing from your life, and the strong feelings that surface when you reflect on what you haven't had the time to do.

- What do you feel guilty about missing?
- What do you feel resentful about not being able to do?
- Who are you sad about, who you never get to see? Who do you never get to see because of your work schedule?

Once you're clear on what's missing, set intentional time for each thing and put it on the calendar. Start with one thing you can schedule each week (yoga class, for example), one thing you can plan to do each month (maybe that's a date night), one thing you can do quarterly (like a networking meeting), and one thing you can do each year (such as a vacation with loved ones).

Coordinate with the involved parties and put these priorities on your calendar.

Use the Time You've Earned

Amira Barger is a vice president at a global communications agency. She is serious about using her paid time off (PTO) and takes one Monday each month as a mental health day to remind herself to recharge.

"I started my 'Mental Health Monday' practice in 2019 right before the pandemic. I was traveling weekly for work on a plane and, as an anxious flyer, I needed to ground myself in a practice. I also wanted to 'spend down my PTO' and ensure that the days I earned were spent and not 'gifted' back to the company, if you will," she said.

Barger says that too many professionals miss using their PTO and she didn't want to be one of them. Instead, she wanted to end each year with a zero PTO balance, mainly to force herself to rest.

She generally uses the days to take a nap or to visit a national park near water.

If you have unused PTO, what's stopping you from using more of it? How can you get more intentional like Barger, of spending it down more each year?

How to Create a Personal Culture of Rest and Sabbatical

Steven Hughes is a financial therapist who says the last two years have fundamentally changed his approach to work. That includes prescheduled time off.

"Since the pandemic, I've taken a different approach to be sure I operate at my best for the clients I work with. Before, I focused on a ton of activity and action. Now I focus, first, on how I can be my best self and show up at the very top of my capabilities to get them the best results. I've found that those results are most predictable when I'm not overwhelmed, stressed, or the like. Mental health days have allowed me to show up better at work."

Hughes has accountability in his sister, who is a huge advocate for mental health. "She's always telling me to take more days off," Hughes said.

At one point things picked up with his business and opportunities were coming at him fast in the form of speaking engagements and new client leads. He was happy for the opportunity but felt overwhelmed by all he needed to do to rise to the occasion. "To keep myself from drowning in opportunity, I took a week off of work," Hughes said. "Now I take a week off every quarter."

You may not be able to take a week off every quarter, but you can do something every quarter. The idea is to create a personal culture in which you prioritize your time off to rest and reset. Could that look like one half-day off once per month to start? Could it be coming into work later in the morning once per week? Consider what would be most helpful to you and what would work best for your situation, and start experimenting with time alignment.

Key Insights

- If you want to escape machine mindset for good, you'll have to stop ignoring your needs and start tuning in to your body, mind, and emotional self. Alignment in this area will mean that you will have to get intentional about how you spend your time. There will always be someone who has their own ideas about how your time should be used to their benefit.

- Vacation, PTO, mental health days, and sabbaticals are not luxuries. They are necessities that allow for the important and necessary work of winter. Remember, observing winter sets you up for success in the other seasons.

- When you make time for energy-generating relationships and energy-generating activities like regular exercise, hobbies, and friends, you gift yourself the energy you need to see your way out of burnout.

- When you decide to use your time in new ways, you may have to defend your new choices and boundaries. Prepare yourself to manage the responses of people who may or may not be supportive.

- Bringing your time back into alignment is energizing.

12 | Restore and Realign Space

The fourth way to bring yourself back into alignment and begin to reduce the energy-draining friction that contributes to burnout is to realign your nervous system inputs by bringing your sensory experience, your space, and your sense of place into focus.

How you reclaim will differ for everyone, but will typically include these actions:

- Reacquaint yourself with nature because earth is your home. Schedule screen detoxes and gadgets diets in favor of nature – aim to replace screen time with green time.
- Be intentional with your senses and reclaiming their power. Reclaim your stillness with a practice.
- Reduce clutter.

Coming home to yourself and honoring your human needs necessitates that you acknowledge you are not a machine. By slowing down, and listening to and caring for yourself, you can begin to better understand what you need to thrive so you can bring yourself into alignment.

In my reporting for this book, one term kept popping up over and over from the people I interviewed: "nervous system." Everyone who had experienced burnout, even temporarily, and come through to the other side mentioned a noticeable difference in their nervous system.

Once Stacey Ferguson stepped away from her company and gave herself a chance to slow down, connect with old friends, and travel, she felt her nervous system begin to reset.

After she left the demanding pace of daily journalism, L'Oreal Thompson Payton found that her anxiety lessened. "I don't know if freelance is forever but right now it's the best scenario for my nervous system, and that's something that I'm really leaning into in this season." When she met with her coach to figure out next steps, her coach told her to keep it simple – get coffee with friends and get back into her morning workout routine. "Basically, she was telling me to sit my [ass] down. She told me I needed to take a beat, that I cannot recover from burnout overnight." This was something Payton needed to hear because, as she describes herself, she has a very driven, ambitious personality type.

Myleik Teele said, "I always have sort of worked out, but now, back when I used to work out and do that business, I'd have to be back at my desk in time for a first meeting, and now I can go to the gym later. So I get up, I get to spend the morning with my kids, I make breakfast sometimes. But I get to have that time with my kids in the morning, and I go to the gym, I get to read, I get to do my podcast. I get to just be a little bit more chill. My nervous system is probably calm. I still work. I do some stuff for another company. I do my podcast consulting, but it's in the parenting space. So I think that part is fun because it's the work that I enjoy."

How Your Nervous System Is Impacted by Burnout

Dr. Aza Allsop is a neuroscientist and psychiatrist at Yale University School of Medicine who studies sound's impact on the nervous system. He told me that burnout becomes a nervous system issue.

"Most people who are struggling with something like burnout have an overactive sympathetic nervous system. They're operating under high stress for extended periods of time with very little time for rest and recharging, essentially, which is what the parasympathetic nervous system does," he explained. "And so when you look at conditions like anxiety, when you look at conditions like even dementia, you can see these imbalances in the autonomic nervous system."

I experienced something fishy around the nervous system myself. At the height of my burnout season, I found myself irritable and overstimulated. But when I'd get up at 3 a.m. with my newborn, I'd stay up after she'd fallen back to sleep. I found that the early morning silence and lack of stimulation seemed to help.

Be Intentional with Your Senses: The Power of Sound

It turns out that the sensory information we're processing at all times is a lot! For me, the competing stimulation of what I might be seeing, hearing, smelling, or sensing at any given moment had me on edge. Pile on top that the 70,000 thoughts going through my head in one day, and my brain and nervous system were fried. I liken it to a computer running with too many applications open, or a system that's trying to perform with too little storage. You know when your computer starts to heat up and the fan comes on, you're in trouble. Processing and response speeds slow down and sometimes applications suddenly quit. For me, that was the sensory experience of burnout. The more I had on my plate with work and family, the more stillness I required to be okay.

I soon realized, however, that silence 24 hours a day was unrealistic, so I started exploring different ways to bring that silence, that stillness into my regular working hours. To start, I began journaling with more intention and consistency. I have been journaling for the most part since my teenage years, but I found a certain time of day to do it and blocked out at least 30 minutes in my calendar before my day began. That really helped.

I discovered singing bowls when a friend introduced me to them in her home. I thought the bowls were interesting and made a fun sound, so I ordered my own set and let my kids "play them" off and on. This wasn't with any real intention and I didn't integrate sound baths into my life with any regularity, but when I heard a podcast interview with Sara Auster, a sound therapist, about the power of sound bathing on one of my favorite podcasts, I was intrigued to give regular sound baths a try.

According to Auster's website, a sound bath is "a deeply immersive, full-body listening experience that intentionally uses sound to invite gentle yet powerful therapeutic and restorative processes to nurture your mind and body. The experience begins with each person lying down or seated in a comfortable position, often with a blanket and an eye mask. After a few minutes of guided focus on the breath, the remainder of the experience is filled with different sounds and frequencies being introduced in succession. The sounds are created by a variety of overtone-emitting instruments, including tuning forks, gongs, a shruti box, Himalayan and crystal singing bowls, chimes, and voice."

I started adding Auster's 20-minute sound baths into my morning routine before I journaled. The sound created a stillness I could hold on to for a bit longer. I found listening to sound baths a way to meditate without meditating, if you will. I could focus on the sounds I was hearing and not worry about clearing my mind completely.

In his neuroscience and psychiatry work, Dr. Allsop is studying how sound impacts our moods. His hope is to eventually be able to medically prescribe certain sounds in the form of music and playlists for healing. He says that while the science is nascent, there seems to be evidence that sound therapy – whether through music, listening to binaural beats, or a sound bath – can heal.

"I do think that sound baths do help and work, especially when the person facilitating them is experienced," said Dr. Allsop. He admits there hasn't been as much research in the form of randomized controlled trials and the evidence is not as robust. But in his opinion, knowing what we do know about sound and subjective reports of their experience with sound baths, they are a tool that can work for healing.

"It's this idea of using very specific frequencies and tonalities within a certain context to help people find a deeper state of relaxation, which activates the parasympathetic nervous system, which in and of itself is the body's own natural mechanism for resting, recharging and healing," he told me.

While you may not be sold on sound baths for healing, you have probably used sound to alter your nervous system without knowing. For example, I use an upbeat playlist to get myself through long drives. According to Allsop, high-tempo music can activate the sympathetic nervous system, enhancing performance during workouts or other physically demanding activities.

"Studies show that music can help people work out longer and lift heavier weights because it activates the sympathetic nervous system," he said. "This is why militaries often use drum lines to prepare soldiers for battle."

So if we are already using sound to help us perk up or calm down, it would make sense that we could harness the power of sound to heal, lower stress levels, and improve overall well-being.

"Sound is interacting with the body on many different levels," he explained. The auditory system processes sound, integrating it into different networks in the brain that are involved in reward, social information processing, and more. The nucleus accumbens, for instance, releases dopamine in response to music, making the experience of listening to music pleasurable and rewarding."

Due to its communicative aspect, music is also considered a language. Musicians, especially in genres like jazz, often refer to music as a language, with specific chords, phrasings, and timing conveying distinct messages. "If you can hit the right chords at the right tempo and timing, you activate certain brain frequencies," Dr. Allsop says.

One of the most crucial aspects of music is its ability to integrate the central and peripheral nervous systems. "Music can very directly, for instance, increase parasympathetic drive to decrease one's heart rate, and decrease one's release of certain stress hormones," Allsop explained. "Music can act on the hypothalamus to decrease the hypothalamus-pituitary-adrenal axis, which leads to less cortisol, which is really important in terms of our stress response."

In other words, the right sounds can cause positive changes within the body, and over time can become valuable interventions for one's nervous system.

Develop a Morning Routine

Kailei Carr supports a community of women and her clients with coaching around their wellness. It started after she watched her mother burn out spectacularly. Carr's mother was a corporate executive who repeatedly skipped winter and burned the candle at both ends for years. A smoker and "night owl," she often worked into the night and subsisted on less than six hours of sleep each day. She didn't exercise.

Although her mother was giving and highly spiritual, Carr says she had no well-being practices, and her spirituality and kindness were not enough to offset the poor health behaviors eroding her overall wellness. Carr watched as her mother's poor health caught up with her and she passed away at the age of 68.

Now Carr is on a mission to help other women find ways to achieve and be well so they don't have the same experience her mother did. One of her key practices is the morning routine she stumbled upon in 2018.

Prior to that, she'd been leading a morning routine challenge on Facebook using Hal Elrod's book *The Miracle Morning*. She'd discovered the book at the end of 2014, going into a year where she knew that she had some really big goals, and that to achieve all of these great things, she had to do things differently. Finding that book was pivotal for her.

For four years, she led a 30-day Miracle Morning challenge every January with her Facebook group of over 200 people. But in 2018, she felt like it wasn't landing the same.

"It's a six-step morning routine. I think it wasn't landing for a few reasons," Carr told me. "I felt like each of the elements were really good—silence, affirmations, visualization, exercise, reading, and journaling, or scribing. But I didn't feel like there was intentionality on the why or what sequence."

She says that following the Miracle Morning routine took her about an hour each day, which was challenging for her as an entrepreneur with a toddler. So she created her own version and called it CLAAIM. This stands for Calm your mind, Lift your energy, Appreciate, Affirm, Intention, and Make it happen (or Manifest).

While she was in the middle of one of her monthly January challenges, the idea for CLAAIM came to her. She decided to switch things up on the fly. She told her group they didn't have to change, but she was going to pivot to make her morning routine fit her schedule better.

"Each step builds on the previous one," she explained. The C stands for calming your mind, which could be as simple as taking a few mindful breaths, listening to your breath go in and out, and allowing yourself to center.

The L is for lifting your energy to a high frequency where things start to happen. She recommends thinking about a time when you were really in the zone. For her, it's memories like her daughter or her wedding day. Our bodies and brains can't tell the difference between what we visualize and what we experience.

The first A is for appreciate, and the second A is for affirm. "There's a lot of science that talks about the benefits and power of gratitude," she said. "Gratitude is a higher-vibration practice or emotion. It builds on lifting your energy by thinking about things you're grateful for, whether big or small."

Affirmation, she clarifies, isn't just about positive affirmations like proclaiming how amazing you are. "It's more about affirming my gifts, who I am, why I'm here, and my purpose," she said.

The I stands for intention. What are your intentions for the day? "I envision myself putting my head on the pillow at the end of the day and I think about how I want to feel. What do I have planned? What's my ideal outcome for each of those things?" she explained.

Finally, M is for make it happen or manifest. She has a guided meditation that's under eight minutes, but she doesn't need to listen to it anymore because she has her process down. The whole routine takes her about five minutes and she does it before getting out of bed.

Switching her approach from the Miracle Morning process to CLAAIM helped Carr respond more than react. "Shifting between the two felt more realistic for where I was, my life stage, and attainable. I felt like I could actually do it," she said.

She still loves the Miracle Morning and still recommends it to people. But after a while it began to feel like an obligation rather than an energizing practice. "It wasn't giving me what it used to give me, which was energy and accomplishment and all of that. I was operating from such a place of obligation. But my heart wasn't in it anymore. For me, CLAAIM has been a game changer."

She really began to notice the impact CLAAIM was making on her life during the pandemic. In the fall of 2021, her daughter started kindergarten and one morning came into her bedroom early in the morning.

"I was tired. I ended up turning off my alarm and had to get up. So I didn't do [CLAAIM] but I didn't realize that I didn't do it," she said. "I just had to go to get my daughter ready for school. And I was just off, and I remember rushing around for stuff; she was wearing masks at school and we had to run back in to get her mask. Then I called my husband from the car and asked if I'd left her snack on the counter. And he said, what is going on with you? And I realized, oh, I didn't do

CLAAIM. And I didn't realize how much it impacted me personally until I didn't do it that day and saw how off I was."

Carr thought she was holding herself together, but it turns out her morning routine was holding her together the whole time.

Practice Meditation

Faida Fuller is a self-described introvert. As a chief operating officer, she works behind the scenes to ensure things go smoothly in her organization. It's a role out of the spotlight and she prefers it that way. But as she's continued to ascend, she's found leadership to require putting herself out there more.

"As I've grown in my career, I've had to find ways to reclaim that sense of being in my element, even when I'm in situations that feel uncomfortable," Fuller said. One way she's helped herself cope with the demands of work is centering herself by developing a practice around meditation.

When she was 12 or 13, Fuller's mother suggested they meditate together. "She tried to teach me how and I remember vaguely blowing her off," Fuller said. "And although I didn't pick up a practice at that early age, it certainly planted the seed."

When Fuller was in her 20s, she was working in the stressful field of New York commercial banking when she experienced inappropriate behavior in the workplace. At the time she didn't feel empowered to report it. She was early in her career and didn't want to make any waves. But dealing with that situation every day at work added another layer of complexity to her already stressful life.

She pushed through and managed to keep showing up at work despite the discomfort. But one night after work, she had a panic attack. "It was after a long day, and I remember being like, oh my God, this is a panic attack. And I realized I had to do something. And I found a three-day mediation course and I began a practice and it was very helpful and useful."

While she didn't keep the practice up, she says it certainly helped her navigate through that time in her life. So she used it whenever she was experiencing extreme stress or challenge at work or in her personal life.

But she finally hit a wall after being in the high-pressure, male-dominated environment of the competitive New York banking field. She got physically sick. She started having stomach cramps and couldn't keep food down. "My doctor diagnosed me with ulcerative colitis – which is stress-induced – and I had to go on steroids and all kinds of medications," Fuller said.

It was at that point that meditation truly became her anchor. "I knew I needed to develop a practice to reduce stress because it was going to kill me if I did not. And so meditation was the approach I took. I knew I didn't want to be on the prescription drugs, so at 27 I got serious about meditation, and I have had a fairly consistent practice ever since then."

Over the years, meditation has helped Fuller through the stresses of being a new wife, a new mother, and through several career pivots. Then, during the pandemic, she took it a step further and felt the call to share the power of meditation with others. She got trained as a meditation instructor and now teaches meditation through wellness workshops at her organization and on the side with one-on-one clients.

"I've found it helps to really balance the notion of the stories that we tell ourselves," she said. "It helps me to challenge what society says about who I am. It helps me challenge the stories that friends, family, community are telling and the stories I tell myself about who I am. Am I these stories or is there something deeper that I need to discover about myself?"

Fuller says that getting grounded in a stillness practice like meditation and regularly incorporating it into your life will impact everyone and everything you touch.

"For me, being in the C-suite, I'm touching the major decisions and guiding the movements from a centered place that impacts the organization's capacity," she said. "Increased capacity impacts the women around the globe that we support. My meditation practice creates a ripple of impact."

Engineer Your Environment

If we understand that the senses are powerful, why aren't we more intentional about engineering our environments?

Amber Cabral, whom you met at the beginning of the book, began prioritizing weekly practices to help her nervous system heal after her godmother's sudden death left her reeling. She wanted to make supporting changes to her routine that helped her cope with her grief while she managed the day to day of her business. She went down the list and began intentionally engineering her daily experience. She scheduled weekly acupuncture and Reiki sessions – practices she'd used off and on in the past. She also got intentional about her home.

She started to prioritize things that she noticed were really important to her well-being. For her that means always living in a place with west-facing windows so she can view the sunset. She also chooses a place with a deep bathtub so she can take a regular soak. "I was a lot more intentional about using my space. I was a lot more intentional about decorating my space after my godmother passed," she said. "I got a lot clearer about what home needed to look and feel like for me."

So she invested in getting her home to that place. She got intentional about a fitness plan. She started going to acupuncture once every two weeks and Reiki once a week. She added health, rest, and well-being as a company value. It was important for her as an entrepreneur not just to make that value explicit in her personal life but in how she engages with clients because her work is an extension of her.

"If I'm going to be here, it needs to support the values that I have. And because it's my company, I think it's important that these values align."

Reacquaint Yourself with Nature

Like Amber, I've engineered parts of my home to respond to my sensory needs. However, I've found the perfect sensory environment to be a forest full of trees.

When I was navigating my most severe season of burnout to date, I became extremely sensitive to sound. I would wear noise-canceling headphones whenever I left the house so I could plug into soothing music, listen to a podcast, or indulge in a sound bath. I found it helped me keep my nervous system in check.

But the one place I didn't feel the need to wear my AirPods was the forest. The mix of birdsong, trees, and other nature sounds made it the perfect sensory environment for me to heal from burnout.

I grew up in Nashville, Tennessee, in the late 1980s and early 1990s and I vividly remember nature hikes with my mother and brother, where we'd spend hours in the forest several times per month. I didn't realize it then, but the greater Nashville area is overflowing with stunning displays of nature. There are multiple state parks complete with lakes, forests, and mountains – all within short driving distance.

Now, as an adult, I often take my children to nearby Rock Creek Park, or disappear there alone for hours, weather permitting. I realize that my comfort in the forest and my need for time in nature came from my mother. Her love for nature was passed down to her by her family members as well.

If there is any one gift given to me as a child that I will always hold dear it is the experience of spending my summers in the South. Beginning when I was about two years old, my parents sent my brother and me every summer to live with our grandparents in a small town in southern Georgia.

Those summer days were carefree ones that were educational in a way I took for granted. A fig tree stood in the backyard, and though it was forbidden, we still dared to climb it. Tomatoes and okra grew in my grandpa's garden – fresher and sweeter than any produce at the local Piggly Wiggly. My summers in Georgia were rich in ways and for reasons that I was only able to appreciate later. I learned that there is an entire world beyond the city – and, as my dad taught me, if you stand very still in the middle of a pine forest and close your eyes, the wind through the pine needles sounds strangely like the ocean.

I have always loved forests more than any other aspect of nature and consider one of my personal conditions for optimal growth regular time in nature. Growing up in the South I experienced a lot of nature but I didn't realize how much I needed it until I began a regular practice of nature hiking and forest bathing right before the pandemic.

My favorite forest path is very close to my kids' old school. Since I was making the drive to their school daily I figured I would make it worth my while with a daily trip to the forest.

What I didn't anticipate but came to enjoy and rely on were the trees I got to know on my daily walks. Those trees comforted me, were friends to me, and gave me solace and the space to work through whatever challenges or questions I had at the moment. I walked religiously starting in the fall, through the winter, even when there was snow on the ground. I even felt a smugness when the trail thinned out after winter came, and the branches were bare, and only I and a few others were still showing up daily.

When the pandemic forced the children's school to go virtual, it didn't make sense for me to make the daily drive across town to my usual trail. But oh, how I missed my trees! One day I took my sons for a field trip to get out of the house, and while I waited for them I spent a few hours in the forest. As I walked and saw the trees, I wondered if they had missed me. I missed them so much. And because we were visited that particular summer by cicadas, they had a new and unusual chorus to seemingly welcome me home. It should have been no surprise to me how important those forest hikes were to me, as time in nature could be considered a prescription for burnout.

Ecotheraphy is an umbrella term that includes therapies and activities based in nature designed to improve one's mental health. But even if you're not under a doctor's care while outside, science has shown a clear correlation between time in nature and lowered stress, decreased anxiety, and improved well-being.

The bottom line is that nature is something to appreciate and engage with, something that heals. Nature makes deposits into your nervous system's bank account, increasing your margin for and ability to handle stress.

But communing with nature is only one way to reset your nervous system. I'm a firm believer in finding the stillness practice that works for you. For my husband, an intense workout with headphones on is his ideal practice. For me, a sound bath followed by a walk in the forest is heaven. For my mom, a 60-minute yoga class and daily gardening hold her nervous system together.

Engage in Breathwork

One tool we all have access to but don't fully utilize as a stillness practice is the breath. Kiesha Yokers is a somatic coach specializing in breathwork who helps clients heal their trauma.

She says there are both mental and physical benefits of using the breath. Breathing deeply oxygenates your brain and other organs, which can have immediate calming or energizing effects. Whatever you're struggling with, there's a breathwork exercise for that.

"If you need energy, there's breathwork strategies that will energize your body," she said. "And then if you are struggling to sleep, there are breathwork strategies that will help shift your nervous system into your parasympathetic that rest and digest place."

Yokers says there are breathwork exercises for everything from a headache to anxiety, but it's a free tool we all have access to that most of us don't take ample advantage of. Like sound, breathing exercises can help calm the nervous system and, done over time, can add to your overall ability to weather additional stress and cope. When used as a regular practice, like physical exercise, the benefits tend to accumulate.

Starting small is key to integrating breathwork into your daily routine. Since not everyone has equal opportunities for peace and quiet, start with just a few minutes – trying to do more may actually make you more anxious.

For beginners, Yokers recommends starting with five minutes or less. "We're busy, and we don't want to feel like it's another burden. The best time for breathwork might be in bed in the morning, at the end of the day, or you might need to set an alarm. Just three to five minutes of slow breathing can make a difference. If you forget everything else, remember to breathe through your nose, low and slow into your belly."

Yokers advises beginning with awareness: "Start by noticing how you're breathing. Shift to breathing through your nose, then aim to breathe deeply into your belly. Slowing down the exhale longer than the inhale can calm your heart rate."

For those experiencing severe depression or immobilization, Yokers suggests more activating practices like short daily walks, even just two minutes, to stimulate your body safely. Sunshine and movement are crucial.

For managing stress and burnout, Yokers recommends simple techniques like box breathing. "Box breathing involves inhaling through your nose for four counts, holding for four, exhaling for four, and holding again for four." This form of breathwork is a technique used by Navy SEALs to calm their heart rates during missions and can be incredibly effective. You can use it, too.

If at all possible, try to find a personal, quiet space for breathwork. "For me, it's my closet," Yokers says. "I love to go into my closet – it's the only place people just leave me alone. I can just sit on the floor. I actually have a meditation cushion, and I don't have candles lit because I'm not a candle person. It's cold in there, and I like that feeling. I put my cushion down and I sit on it and for five minutes I just breathe."

Journaling briefly after a breathwork session can be helpful and though she says she doesn't love journaling, she spends a minute to jot down her thoughts in order to notice herself and pay attention to her body's signals.

Breathwork is so powerful and accessible to everyone that Yokers has even taught her kids to do it. "My kids know a lot of different breathwork, and it's taught them to be aware of their state," she said. "My seven- and nine-year-old will say, 'I'm in anxious state,' and they know how to use breath work to help shift that."

By starting small and gradually building up, anyone can incorporate breathwork into their daily routine, leveraging this powerful tool to enhance overall wellness and resilience to stress.

Reduce Clutter

On a recent Sunday morning, I found myself sitting in silence by a crackling fire in a white-walled room of a modest brick home in the northeast quadrant of Washington, DC. It had snowed the day before, and a blanket of white powder coated the ground outside. It was beautiful. Peaceful. Serene.

I and a handful of women had been invited to this house for a session of "communal rest."

Once inside, I removed my shoes and took off my coat before venturing in to find a cozy space to camp out for the next hour. I found my spot in a corner on the couch, right in front of a fire. I settled in.

Over the next 60 minutes I absorbed a soothing playlist – sound bath or binaural beats – as I downloaded the week's events into my journal. I had a lot to get off my chest, and for some reason (even though my husband and children were out and about in the city) my house didn't feel very restful. But this space was distraction-free.

One woman sat upright on the floor. One woman took over a chair and periodically scribbled into her journal. Another woman got under a blanket and slept.

After the hour was up, a bell chimed three times, signaling to us that the experience was officially over. We assembled and shared our thoughts on what came up for us during the hour of silence.

Trisha Hersey – aka the Nap Bishop of the popular online account the Nap Ministry – inspired thousands of people during the pandemic. Her simple and repeated calls for rest felt revolutionary for a group of people who judged their worth by their work output.

Hersey introduced many to the idea that rest is our birthright, and we don't have to earn the opportunity to take time out to dream. She popularized the idea of communal rest, sharing photos of her congregation members (followers) mass napping together.

This idea of communal rest inspired Imani Samuels to found HURU Space and host gatherings like these for community members to come together. I wasn't sure what to expect from a community rest session. But I was pleasantly surprised by how energizing it was to rest . . . together.

But I think I was even more taken by the communal resting environment Samuels had created for our group. As I glanced around the room that was sparsely furnished and free from distractions, I realized that even without a person in my home making requests on my time, the sheer volume of mental triggers made true rest and mental clarity difficult to achieve. At home, I felt assaulted with reminders of tasks undone. I found myself in a constant state of low-grade anxiety as I made mental lists and cataloged dwindling supplies. I was exhausted by my stuff.

I didn't realize how much my stuff triggered thoughts of a cosmic internal computer overheating. Being in a space that was sparsely populated, and had none of my things, helped me to disconnect. I felt my shoulders fall as I observed the clean slate of my environment. There were no triggers, no reminders, nothing to add to my cognitive load.

The field of minimalism is a growing movement that encourages individuals to lessen their impact on the environment by getting rid of most of their things. I can definitely understand how having fewer items in my surroundings could help me with burnout. By wearing a uniform, I could cut down on the daily decisions of what to wear. By having certain books on my shelf, I could cut down on the idea that I need to choose what to read next.

There are many ways to approach minimalism. I would not call myself a minimalist as of yet, especially given that I am in the thick of child-rearing. However, when I am in nature, or somewhere that has none of my belongings, I can feel my load lighten considerably.

Could paring down and/or removing clutter be a key to creating more mental margin for you?

Curb your screen time regularly with scheduled screen detoxes. Schedule screen detoxes and gadgets diets in favor of forest time – aim to replace screens with green.

Often when I'm sitting at my desk, I have my iPad open for research, my desktop machine up and running while I type, and my phone within reach so I can see text messages and emails. I'm not unique – screen usage has increased dramatically since I first entered the workforce. And among young people, screens are increasingly required in the classrooms instead of paper textbooks, and online communication through screens is young people's primary way to keep in touch.

But excessive screen use can lead to eye strain, headaches, and other ailments. To combat this, I've noticed numerous people announcing social media hiatuses, giving up social media for Lent or scheduling screen detoxes and gadget diets at regular intervals throughout the year.

Perhaps because I personally have such powerfully healing experiences in nature, whenever possible I try to swap screen time for green time to help make deposits into my nervous system. Studies show that being outdoors can reduce stress, boost your mood, and improve your overall well-being, so whenever I can get away from all of my screens and spend some time in nature, I do.

The practice of "forest bathing" (*shinrin-yoku* in Japan) involves spending time in the forest and has tons of health benefits, like lowering blood pressure, reducing stress hormones, and boosting your immune system.

To get started, plan to set aside screen-free times in your calendar. You may start out with an hour before bed without screens and work your way up to a full day offline every week. During these times, swap screen time for outdoor activities like walking in the park, hiking a forest trail, or just sitting outside.

I live in a busy urban area and I'm not always able to escape to my forest trail. However, I have a small outdoor space behind my house that I've equipped with a windchime for an old-school sound bath whenever there's a breeze. There is a small patch of grass next to the patio; there are a few trees that attract squirrels and birds. I work from home and find that when I'm able to go back there in the middle of the day, have a seat, listen to the birds and feel the sunshine on my face, it helps.

I think it's important to note that my preference would of course be a two-mile hike through a specific wooded trail. But if I only have 20 minutes, my patch of grass will do in a pinch.

Key Insights

- People struggling with burnout typically have overactive sympathetic nervous systems that have been under the weight of tremendous stress over extended periods of time.
- One of the easiest way to heal the nervous system and detangle from machine mindset is to spend time in nature. Nature is healing to humans because we are beings of nature.
- Stillness practices like gardening, meditation, sound baths, or journaling are important tools for recalibrating one's nervous system after burnout. The healing effects of regular stillness are both immediate and cumulative over time.
- The breath is a tool anyone can use at any time to calm the nervous system, yet the breath is an underutilized tool for most people.
- Clutter can increase your cognitive load, further burden your nervous system, and add to feelings of exhaustion. Minimalism is a growing movement that those suffering with burnout may want to consider.

13 | Restore Your Connections

The fifth and final way we'll explore to bring yourself back into alignment and begin to reduce the energy-draining friction that contributes to burnout is to restore your connection with others. Isolation drains, but connection fuels.

Restoring your connection with others will differ for everyone, but will typically include these actions:

- Auditing your existing connection to see where the energy lies
- Bringing your focus back on high-quality connections and relationships and rekindling energy-generating relationships that have been deprioritized
- Seeking out like minds and communities
- Building rituals and scheduling regular time for connection with energy-generating relationships
- Establishing a support structure

Honoring your human need for connection is another way to break the chokehold of machine mindset. By slowing down and acknowledging your feelings of disconnection and loneliness, you can begin to better understand the connection and support you need so that you may bring yourself into alignment.

Loneliness: How Your Social Bonds Impact Burnout

Scientists at the University of Vienna conducted a study in 2023 that connected loneliness and social isolation to fatigue. During their study, they found that being socially isolated can leave people feeling overly tired and drained. "Social isolation led to lowered self-reported energetic arousal and heightened fatigue, comparable with food deprivation," the report stated. "Social contact is considered a basic need in many animals, and, like our need for food, it may be governed by a dedicated regulatory system referred to as 'social homeostasis.'"

The drop in energy levels witnessed during the study suggest that fatigue could be part of the body's response to the lack of social contact. So how does this connect to burnout? For individuals who are already navigating the friction produced by misaligned ambitions, use of their time, inauthenticity, and an unregulated nervous system, loneliness may push their resilience to the limit.

Recent studies have also shown that, unfortunately, more than half of US adults are lonely. But people from underrepresented racial groups, people with incomes less than $50,000 per year, and adults aged 18–34 are even lonelier. Members of these groups report feeling "left out" at higher rates than their counterparts, according to a study commissioned by Cigna at the end of 2021.

Loneliness does not discriminate between genders; both men and women report being lonely at about the same rates.

Exhaustion aside, a majority of Americans understand their social bonds to be a key element to personal success and happiness. According to Pew Research Center, 61% of US adults say having close friends is key to living a fulfilling life, but 40% of adults say they have fewer than three close friends.

How Did We Get So Lonely?

American culture's prioritization of work may be partly to blame. Starting in the 1950s, we more regularly moved away from families and communities of origin to chase career and educational opportunities. Both of my parents were born in 1948 in small Southern towns with fewer than 10,000 residents. They moved from their respective towns to Nashville, Tennessee, to attend Tennessee State University in 1966, and then never left the Nashville area. I grew up there but missed out on the experience of having local grandparents and nearby cousins who weave an early fabric of built-in social connection.

When televisions first became staples of American households, our mode of socializing and entertaining shifted once again. Club involvement and communal gatherings declined as televisions in the home became more widespread in the late 1950s and early 1960s. More people found amusement and gained a new perspective of the world through their television screens.

Fast-forward several decades, and the digital revolution kicked this phenomenon into overdrive. We now carry around tiny screens in the form of smartphones and never have to engage with our fellow humans if we do not want to.

Work and parenting duties compound loneliness when discretionary time is taken up with those responsibilities. With more of us living in different cities, states, and even countries from our families of origin, the lack of automatic support with child-rearing and caretaking that used to be the purview of grandparents, aunts, and uncles is shouldered by the nuclear familial unit unless new support networks are developed.

It's a vicious cycle. We're busier than ever and need more support to keep it all going, but we struggle to find time to maintain relationships and build new connections, which means we are lonelier.

All of this conspires to add to the load of burnout. Our social needs and our social realities are woefully misaligned. That misalignment in the kinds and amounts of connection we need and what we actually receive creates friction and causes energy leaks that eventually pave the way to burnout.

The solution to loneliness – and the energy leaks caused by social misalignment – is more connection. But if so many people are lonely and too busy to do anything about it, where do we start?

Inevitably, at some point in your journey you'll look up and realize you do not have as many friends or supportive colleagues as you'd like to have. If having close friendships and connections is more important to you than having a lot of money, how can you proactively close the connection gap after a relocation, career pivot, or the friendships you built earlier in life have run their course?

How Social Gaps Leave Us Vulnerable to Loneliness

Monday, May 7, 2018, is a day I'll never forget. I can remember so clearly; it was a beautiful sunny day. After doing some thinking and writing, I headed to a coffee shop in Takoma Park right outside of Washington, DC, where I met weekly with my dear friend Tara to get our week started. Earlier that morning, I had sent out a newsletter to my email list about the pain I experienced of standing out for being a brainiac in the second grade.

On the drive over Tara emailed me in response: "This needs to be the opening chapter to Package Your Genius adults or kids. This had me almost in tears. I know this feeling all too well and I am sure others could relate too!"

When Being Yourself Is "Doing Too Much"

When I got to the coffee shop, Tara was on the phone, so I got in line to order my standard cafe au lait. With coffee in hand, I made my way over to the table where she was sitting. She hung up her call and greeted me warmly, as she always did. Her face lit up and she smiled before asking me if I'd gotten her email response. I told her that I had, and thought that it would end there.

With eyes watering, she went on to share with me the visceral reaction she'd had to my words and how she felt similarly as a gifted child in classrooms that catered to mediocrity. She actively affirmed my talent. I was somewhat surprised because she rarely gushed about anything; as a former marketing executive, she'd seen it all. She was tough to impress, so a compliment from her – particularly one this glowing – was rare.

So I soaked it in. I thought about what she said, circled back to our previous discussions about getting the Package Your Genius concept in front of children, in the way my children have ready access to it at home with me. Earlier that year, when my then-fourth-grade son, Connor, wrote what I thought was a pretty good story and I told him I'd help him publish it, Tara was the first person I ran the idea by. When I asked her if I should proceed to use all of my professional muscle to help him and his book project shine, she encouraged me not to hold back. When the slim paperback book proof came in the mail, she was one of the first people I showed it to. I remember feeling a twinge of excitement but nervousness about the whole thing. "I mean, he's nine," I told her. "Is this too much?"

She affirmed that I was not in fact "doing too much" by helping get a nine-year-old's story printed and available for sale on Amazon. She assured me that this would do wonders for his confidence and sense of self.

Everything she'd said about the book had been right – as her counsel generally was. So on this day in the coffee shop as she affirmed me, I listened. She asserted that my work was needed now more than ever. She reminded me how early messages from well-meaning teachers or misguided parents all have the power to shift your journey, throw off your confidence, and make you second-guess yourself.

As the morning turned into afternoon, we packed our things and moved our meeting from the coffee shop to a nearby restaurant and ordered lunch. I had a full calendar of client calls that afternoon so I ate quickly in order to depart for a quieter place to take my calls. I had already started one call before lunch ended so I got up from our outdoor table at the restaurant and signaled that I was leaving before heading to my car.

I had no idea that would be the last time I would see her. I got the news the next day that sometime in the hours after our meeting, my friend had passed away.

Her death left a gaping, sister-sized hole in my life that, to be honest, I still have not filled. But I often think back to our last conversation. I can hear her voice affirming me, encouraging me to get over myself and stop holding back my ideas. She was the kind of friend who would let you know how impressed she was by you – instead of displaying jealousy or encouraging you to dim anything, she was the hype woman who encouraged you to take it to the next level, to think bigger, to be more of your authentic self.

Her friendship was energizing. Everyone should have a friend like that. Everyone should have a weekly meeting with their own hype person. Everyone should have at least one person who believes in their talent, and encourages them to believe more in it, too.

Audit Your Existing Connections to See Where the Energy Lies

Just as there are certain activities that generate the energy we can tap into to help us climb out of burnout, relationships have the power to do the same. I call these EGRs – energy-generating relationships. My friend was a powerful example of an EGR and helped me realize the criteria for what that looked like in my life.

Do you have enough EGRs? Are you the EGR to other people in your life when they mostly drain you? Examine your connections – family members, friends, co-workers, colleagues, and collaborators – and determine who energizes you. Who do you feel excited to talk to and share your latest discovery? With whom can you share your most personal interests and hobbies?

Years ago, I once rode a bus from Washington, DC, to New York City with less than 24 hours notice to see a Romare Bearden collage on its final day hanging in the Metropolitan Museum of Art. When I asked my friend Johnica if she wanted to take the ride with me, she immediately said yes and we had a fantastic, spontaneous art- and culture-filled day that was energizing beyond measure.

Who'd be willing to take a last-minute field trip with you in service of one of your passions? Who, like my friend Tara, encourages you to be more of yourself? Who listens to you and gives you feedback that helps you grow? Those are your EGRs.

Once you know who your EGRs are, you need to ensure they are getting the bulk of your time. Look at your calendar, your emails, and text messages. Who are you spending time with or communicating with the most, outside of the people you are responsible to and for? Do your EGRs make the list? Or is your discretionary time filled to the brim with people who deplete you rather than fill you up?

If that's the case, it's time to make some changes about which relationships get the prioritization of your time and attention.

The good news is, if you know who energizes you but you aren't currently making time for them, there's opportunity there. You have the power to make the changes that can bring you more energy and fulfillment; you just have to get intentional about connecting more regularly.

From Doer to Leader Comes Down to Support

One of the ways social disconnection shows up in the workplace for high achievers is the tendency to go it alone instead of seeking out the support one may need. For underrepresented groups, this can be a coping mechanism and a way to ward off misconceptions that they did not earn their seat at the table. But trying to do it all or know it all can backfire.

After Quiana Smith got promoted, her job description didn't change much. The biggest change came in the form of a team to help with the workload. While her new role came with support baked in, she says it took some time to accept it. First she had to break her personal pattern of overworking and overextending herself to prove her value.

"I think a lot of us feel like asking for or needing help shows weakness. And now out of the gate, I know I need help. I'm not here to do it all. I'm not here to be it all. I have no desire whatsoever in any aspect of my life to be that person, to be that superwoman or to be society's view of a boss. None of that is appealing to me."

Now Smith does not just accept support from others – she demands it. But that can look different depending on the situation. "The way I set the tone for my team is that I view myself as who I truly am at the core. I am a visionary, I'm a strategist, I'm an innovator. So now I get to do that, to drive the ship. In order to execute on those strategies, I need my team to do that. But also it's my responsibility to understand what the aspirations are of each person on my team so that I help him or her get to that."

She now judges herself as a leader by the degree to which she's able to empower her team members to grow and reach their career goals. She works to assign them responsibilities not just because she does not want to do them, but because they need the responsibility to brand themselves properly, and get the experience and expertise they need to build a career. So she's traded in her old need to know all of the answers for leveraging other people's knowledge. She now surrounds herself with subject matter experts whom she can learn from.

"I'm going to ask you to partner with me to build that because that is your area of expertise, because it makes no sense for me to go and do this research and wear myself out about something that I'm not familiar with. And quite honestly, I'm not even interested in when you have that information," she explained.

One of the biggest ways Smith has started to step into leadership without overworking is releasing perfection and the need to know everything. "That's why relationships are so important because I need to know people who know stuff that I do not know," she said. "I do not have time to be Encyclopedia Britannica. I have no interest in being that. And so I need to leverage other people's knowledge and establish relationships and partnerships that are reciprocal."

To accept support, she had to ultimately let go of control. But not being in control somehow feels smarter. "To me, that's much more of an intelligent move than sitting in the corner pretending like you know something that you do not know," Smith said. "You're wasting your time and you are wasting everybody else's time."

Double Down on High-Quality EGAs

The World Health Organization declared loneliness a "pressing health threat," and launched a new commission to foster social connection as a priority in all countries (https://www.who.int/news/item/15-11-2023-who-launches-commission-to-foster-social-connection).

But loneliness does not impact all groups equally. According to a study done by Cigna and Morning Consult, loneliness disproportionately impacts people of color. Seventy-five percent of Hispanic adults and 68% of Black/African American adults are classified as lonely, compared to 58% of the total adult population.

Christina Ricks Canty's mother shared Thanksgiving tales of years gone by when her own parents would get all dressed up to attend their university's homecoming on Thanksgiving Day. Back then, the homecoming day would start with a gathering, followed by the football game, followed by a group Thanksgiving dinner. By the time Canty herself was of age, the homecoming game was no longer on Thanksgiving Day, but the tradition of communal celebration remained.

"When I finally went to the [Thanksgiving] cocktail party as a teenager, I got to see a bit of the fun," recalls Canty fondly. "I remember a beautiful hotel ballroom, fur coats, dancing, table rounds, conversations, and a large band. It was a gathering to look forward to."

Years later, Canty – now a Washington, DC–based marketing director, wife, and mother – began hosting an annual holiday gathering of her own on the evening before Thanksgiving at a lounge or restaurant in Washington, DC. Canty brings together a cross-section of her college friends, past and present neighbors, volunteer service organizations – a mixture of people who all mean something to her. She started her annual "Toast to Friendship" in 2012.

"I was in my early 30s, solidly in early adulthood but not yet in a family unit – and there was no guarantee that I would go that route – so I wanted to create a warm tradition of my own," Canty said. "It was also a nod to the way I remember my grandparents celebrating Thanksgiving. For my grandparents and their community, Thanksgiving was a time for fellowship with the larger community."

The holidays are a natural point of the year to take stock of relationships and shore up personal connections. But that's not the only time.

For Kailei Carr, community and connection are year-round affairs. Carr, who shared her morning routine with us in Chapter 12, is the CEO and founder of the Beyonding Community of "purpose-driven, high-achieving women who are all on a journey toward greater well-being and self-actualization." Carr founded the community online in 2020 after she was unable to host an in-person retreat during the pandemic. Initially a three-month experience with experts, coaches, and storytellers, it was meant to spark individual healing, growth, and support during a tumultuous time.

"We were meeting every other week during that time frame and I felt really strongly that we needed to have an online platform to keep us connected in between sessions," said Carr. "As context, the majority of the women in the initial program were Black women, and the first session took place during a weekend of protests surrounding George Floyd's murder. After that initial program was over in August 2020, the women in the program asked if we could keep the community going as it had been a lifeline for so many during that time. What was clear was that these highly successful women were pouring into everyone around them and had nothing left to give."

According to Carr, the ad hoc community gave her women permission to finally receive care and get to know other women who were just like them. So in January 2021, she formalized it as a membership community to create a safe space for her members.

In September 2022, she hosted the first Beyonding Retreat in-person in Arizona. There are currently close to 100 members located in the United States and the Caribbean.

"We are not meant to be in isolation," Carr stated. "During the pandemic, many of us got comfortable with being in our own bubbles, which was necessary to protect our physical health, but has had long-term impact on social connection. Social connection is core to us being human."

But where do we begin?

Make Connection a Priority

Nicole Venable is a lobbyist in Washington. She's constantly in touch with her classmates from Spelman College; she relies on them and considers them family. For her, attending her alma mater's annual homecoming event is a social priority.

"I make it a point to clear my work schedule for homecoming and my class reunion every year," she said. "It's good to go back and be around so much positivity and so much support. I tap into my HBCU [Historically Black Colleges and Universities] network daily in what I do."

Alex Dixon, 42, relies on his college relationships in a similar way. He graduated from Howard University in 2003 and since then has moved around the country nearly a dozen times with his family for work. He now lives in Dubuque, Iowa, where he serves as a CEO. Through the many moves and life changes, one thing that has remained consistent is his affiliation with Howard and his Howard classmates – a connection that sustains him.

"I'm a workaholic," Dixon said. "I can live in a place like Dubuque and my world, for the most part, is in all white spaces. But my connection [to Howard] is always here."

Similarly, Venable says she considers the Spelman and Morehouse alumni community the family she has curated for life. "When we see each other it's all *love*," she declared. "We catch up, but it's also like we just saw each other on campus 30 years ago. When I travel, I always look up my classmates to have a drink. These interactions are sacred and special."

Build Rituals and Schedule Regular Time for Connection

For Canty, intentionally connecting with others is critical. As an only child, she sees her social connections as a second family. She recommends that for those looking to kick off a tradition in their own lives, start with what's authentic to you.

"Think about how you want to connect with people – what spaces feel warm and inviting to you – and start there. By all means, if you love the holidays too and like the community of local bars (think *Cheers*) start a Thanksgiving-Eve Toast to Friendship in your community and do not re-create the wheel," she advises.

Or you can start an annual tradition centered around your hobbies and interests. "If you are feeling disconnected, think about how you can organically be a connector by starting with what moves you. Engage people who want to do the things that you do. You could start a holiday run club and run through the city and end at a local watering hole owned by a small business owner and toast to the freedom to move. Whatever feels authentic to you, do that and make it a recurring thing to give people something to look forward to," she said.

Prioritizing connection is especially critical during midlife. Carr, 47, explains, "What we have seen for women who are in a midlife season, with job and caregiving responsibilities plus the pressures of our communities and the world as a whole, having meaningful relationships and support is critical to our well-being. It is counterintuitive when we feel overwhelmed, but what I've seen is that the outcomes lead to more support, decreased overwhelm, and perspective that allows us to build resilience and keep going."

But she's determined to continue creating spaces for women to connect even when it's hard. There's too much at stake. "Research shows that feelings of loneliness and isolation decrease our lifespan," Carr said. "So this is literally life or death."

Get Clear on Your Interests

If you have recently relocated, had to move for school or work, or switched industries due to layoff or burnout, you are likely overwhelmed and potentially even exhausted. If that's the case, you could probably use a social outlet unrelated to school or work to help you recharge.

Luckily, we all have a natural charging system we can access at any time – our interests, hobbies, and passions. If you have put them on the back burner due to a busy career season, I encourage you to tap back into these natural sources of energy and seek out communities of people who gather around your shared interests. People are generally thrilled to meet others who share their interests and passions – especially if those interests are rare.

What interests have you indulged in, in isolation or put on the back burner altogether? Wherever you are now, try to find a workshop, class, or gathering where people are exploring that interest in community. Once you are in, take note of who you meet.

Tap into Your School History

Even if you were not active on campus, if there's a local alumni group from your university days, it's possibly an automatic network you can tap to get plugged in to new people.

When it comes to school alumni groups, most people only consider who may resurface from their graduating class. But alumni groups welcome members who graduated well before and well after you did. There's bound to be someone in the room whom you did not know when you were in school. And if you tap into class-specific alumni events, there will likely be someone you may have crossed paths with at some point whom you can get to know better now.

When possible, attend events in person. But if there aren't any in-person events coming up in your local area, look for an alumni Facebook or LinkedIn group. There, you can get plugged into quarterly or annual gatherings that may be happening around graduation, convocation days, or homecoming celebrations.

Find Younger People to Mentor and Learn From

If you are starting over or in a position to refresh your network, you likely have some creative or professional skills you have been developing that could be helpful to younger professionals who are just starting out. Do not let those skills go to waste, and more importantly, do not let them atrophy.

Go to local universities, ask about formal mentor match programs in your new organization, or tap into a religious community or place of worship. Let people know you are available to share your knowledge. Seek out opportunities to mentor young professionals who can help you keep your skills sharp, add capacity to your future projects, expose the gaps in your current methods, and keep you up to date on current trends.

As you mature in your career, your network will mature as well. Naturally, your network will shrink as some colleagues retire and leave the workforce. Mentoring can be a great way to keep those numbers in your overall network balanced. By teaching others, you give yourself meaning and purpose, position yourself to meet new people, and put yourself in the mix to be introduced. You are also helping someone else or a group of people get ahead. It's a win-win-win all around.

Figure Out How You Can Serve

Get involved in at least one volunteer organization to give back while meeting new people. If you are making a career pivot, do a little strategic sleuthing. Investigate the people you'd like to eventually connect with in this new industry or organization. Look them up on LinkedIn or search for news about them online. Where are they already involved? What boards do they sit on? Which organizations have given them awards? Which fundraising events do they attend annually?

Once you know which organizations are the go-to organizations for the go-to people in your new industry, see how you can be involved by volunteering, introducing yourself to organization leadership, and showing up for events.

Create a New Community of Your Own

If you have tried tapping into the existing communities around you and you are not quite satisfied, feel free to create the thing you wish existed. Many of the communities that spring up started from one person's desire to connect around an interest or identity they did not see being served in the marketplace.

You're likely seeking to build a network because you do not already have one, so convening others might not be as straightforward as announcing your new gathering to the people you know. Instead, you can start by attending whatever communities do exist and scouting for new members for your group.

For example, if I wanted to create a group for "Moms over 40 who aspire to author books," I might go to existing writing groups to see if I could find moms over 40. I might go to mom groups to look for moms who are writers. I might go to a group of women over 40 and see if any of the women were also moms and writers. You get the idea.

A version of the same approach could be applied online. Facebook groups are a notorious way to build community around shared interests. They're also a great way to determine the market for an interest. Using the strategy I shared above, you could create a group called "Writers and mothers over 40" and see who joins. Build a bit of community online first before taking it to an in-person group.

Create an Intentional Plan for Connection

While these are all strategies you can use to build your network and community, they'll only work for you if you are intentional about growing your network and vulnerable enough to put yourself out there. If you truly desire more connection in your life, decide what you can realistically do on a daily, weekly, monthly, quarterly, and annual basis to bring more connection into your life.

For example, once a week you can text or message one person you have not talked to in a while just to see how they are. Once a week, you can attend a yoga or other class around your personal interest or meet a new acquaintance for coffee or lunch to explore the connection. Each month you might attend an alumni gathering or meet with a group of younger professionals you are mentoring. Quarterly, perhaps, you can gather a group of your newest connections for brunch or dinner in person so everyone can make a new friend. Annually you can plan to attend your industry's big conference, your university's homecoming festivities, or an event tied to your extracurricular interest.

As you can see, this strategy does not take a ton of time, but it does require intention. If you take some time upfront to consider the ways it makes sense for you to deploy your time and invitations strategically, after a few months you will likely have an entirely refreshed network and set of connections.

A Network Success

Myleik Teele overworked for years as the entrepreneur behind popular beauty subscription Curlbox. But when she became a mother she felt isolated by motherhood, and in true Myleik fashion decided to build her own solution. She launched an online community for moms to share resources.

But Teele was no stranger to the power of community. While growing her subscription box business, she started a podcast to share her business and career experiences. The podcast resonated with other women who were looking for mentorship and guidance; many of them were the first in their families to attend college or work in corporate America.

A community naturally sprang up around her episodes as she answered listener questions and engaged with her audience online. She was recently invited to speak by listeners of the podcast – women who had listened while in college and are now in graduate school at institutions like Harvard and Princeton.

"Creating this community, feeding them, and now they are kicking it back to me," Myleik said. She attributes her network success to her willingness to create the things she wished existed. She created communities to have the kind of conversations and participate in the experiences that she would want to be a part of.

"Having friends is one thing. Having family is another thing," Teele said. "But creating your own community or becoming a part of a community that you have a sense of belonging [within] is probably the greatest gift and will heal you beyond words."

Key Insights

- Connection fuels us and loneliness and isolation can drain us and add to our feelings of burnout. In fact, studies show loneliness can lead to feelings of physical fatigue.
- Some connections foster EGRs or energy-generating relationships while others may drain us. Audit your connections to determine which types you have – and need more of – in your life.
- A lack of support could be fueling your burnout. The need to know it all or do it all can lead to overworking – build supportive connections instead.
- Having a true sense of community will require effort and regular tending on your part. If you don't have the sense of connection you need, examine what parts of your network need building up and consider regular traditions to help keep you connected.
- Wherever you feel disconnected in life there are likely old relationships you can reignite or new relationships you can start around your interests, affinity groups, or alumni connections.

14

What's Working

Although burnout has remained in the headlines consistently since the World Health Organization named it an "occupational phenomenon" in 2019, rates of employee burnout continue to rise. A staggering 57% of employees are experiencing at least moderate levels of burnout, according to a recent report from Aflac. Mental health–related leaves of absence were up 33% in 2023 from 2022.

Overwhelmed employees have been largely left to cope with the stresses of work on their own, and more recently wellness practitioners, coaches, and therapists have stepped in to fill the gap. The burnout epidemic has ushered in a surge of private retreats that cater to exhausted professionals seeking organized opportunities simply to rest.

Octavia Raheem runs one such resting opportunity. She became a rest retreat leader, rest coach, and restorative teacher after successfully navigating through her own devastating experience with severe burnout in 2012.

"At the time I had a full-time job and also taught yoga. I practiced yoga and went to classes three to five times a week. Yet it was apparent to me that I needed more than just a class," she explained.

She attended Maya Breuer's yoga retreat and it opened her up to her need for more space and time to reset and restore than a yoga class could provide. She began leading retreats after over a decade of being a yoga and meditation teacher. At the first retreat, the depth of trust, conversations, resonance, and understanding among the people who attended was palpable.

Many women said they could be more than strong. "They could be at ease, let go, and relax."

Beyond her personal retreat experience, seeing and experiencing the impact that retreats had on her clients and community who were leaders in their work, families, organizations, and centers of faith doubly confirmed how important it was to have a place to step away from the frenetic pace and rat race.

While her initial retreats were rooted in yoga, she received feedback over time that women wanted to slow down, relax, and not do the practices that felt like they needed to perform in any specific way. "They performed at work; they didn't come on retreat to do that."

Retreat by retreat, she began to focus primarily on rest and practices that are more restorative. "The exhales in the room deepened."

Imani Samuels, whom we met in Chapter 5, transitioned from her corporate role after her daughter's health scare. She founded HURU – a wellness center that facilitates individual, communal, and corporate stillness retreats for people in deep need of rest.

"We believe that we can approach societal change with very intentional rest," Samuels said. "Doing, especially in excess, is part of the problem. We've mastered 'doing.' This idea of a retreat places a beautiful emphasis on 'being' – a practice we often neglect in current society."

As HURU has grown since 2020 and served women from all over the world, Samuels has observed that the type of women seeking her care fall into three categories: overworked women experiencing everyday stressors that have become debilitating; purpose seekers who are seeking self-care, spiritual growth, or space to dream; and executives, entrepreneurs, and creatives who acknowledge the importance of stillness and need spaciousness to hone their craft.

In relation to her signature offering of solo rest experiences, Samuels observed that one of the most common threads across all of these groups is that many might recognize the need for rest, while also not knowing how to rest. "These two things can co-exist," she said. "Often there's fear from disconnecting or simply resting alone with your thoughts."

On the rise of the rest retreat industry, Samuels notes that many people have awakened to a culture of selflessness, in which they were "conditioned to believe that any consideration for self-care was self-indulgent and evidence of a lack of commitment." She pointed to a Pew study that reported that 55% of individuals are seeking the purpose of life on a weekly basis, and to the US surgeon general's loneliness study, indicating that the lack of social connectedness – a key variable of the scientific theory of happiness – is known to be as detrimental as smoking 15 cigarettes a day.

Although the Great Resignation coincided with the COVID-19 pandemic, social scientist Todd Rose and his colleagues at Populace, a Boston-area think tank, saw the shifts in employee sentiments well before they became headline news. "We felt pretty confident we saw this coming, and I'll tell you why: I think what the 'Great Resignation' gets wrong is people don't want to opt out of work. They want something different from work."

Rose notes that employees weren't leaving the workforce entirely. Instead, they were switching jobs and, from the private opinion research his think tank is most famous for, he understood why. Publicly, most people weren't being truthful about how they felt about work. But through their unique survey instruments, he and his colleagues were able to tease out, among other things, what Americans wanted most out of work.

"What do people want out of work now? What are their trade-off priorities for work? And what you see changing is people really want meaning and purpose, and they want to contribute," he told me. "They want to be able to, quite literally, show up as themselves. And

I feel like it's not that they need work to be everything, but they need work to be a positive part of the life they want to live."

The pandemic on a macro level, combined with personal losses and transitions on the individual level, have more employees examining how they spend the time they have. They want to put their time into what matters most to them. As Rose noted, "I think that you're seeing people being willing to say, look, life's too short. I don't want to do work that's not meaningful to me."

According to Rose, the idea that work should be meaningful is fairly new. Employees traditionally operated under the assumption that work is not supposed to be enjoyable – you show up to do your job so you can get paid and then you can find fulfillment somewhere else. But based on what Rose observed from his research, the tide is changing. Meaning matters.

More interestingly, Rose says that CEOs are reaching out to him more and more to try to understand talent recruitment and retention. They're starting to understand that perks and company prestige aren't all that meaningful if employees aren't engaged in work that is meaningful to them. "It's really about the work they get to do. And so really getting their heads around, if you want to recruit and retain the best people, this idea of it being meaningful work to them is really important."

Because Populace conducts private opinion research, they noticed that attitudes and preferences change in private before they change in public. "We looked at the lives people want to live. Then we looked at what they want out of work. And it started in private moving there in a pretty big way. The thing we knew with these public shocks to the system, like a pandemic, war does this as well, is it tends to clarify values. So people tend to get back to values really quickly because they're like, life's too short."

He said that employees are beginning to clearly understand the importance of knowing what really matters to them so they are in a position to make good choices.

While the pandemic ushered in a wave of introspection, soul-searching, self-improvement, and therapy on the personal level, Rose says company leaders are beginning to understand how they can make changes as well. He is encouraged to see companies starting to recognize where the world and workers are moving. Instead of focusing so much time on wondering what makes people leave their jobs, Rose and his team are now working with major companies to determine why people stay.

"We don't ever ask that question. It turns out you sort of assume not wanting to leave would be the same as [wanting to stay]. And what you see is, consistently, the people who feel like they have purpose and meaning in their work, that they're treated with respect, that they can be themselves with that authenticity aspect, are the people that just want to stay. And it turns out that they end up being better collaborators and better colleagues."

He believes a new vision for work is one that does not have to come at the cost of productivity. "In fact, I think the exact opposite," he said. "We've eked out everything you could get from treating people as widgets. There's no more gains to be made there."

How Workplaces Can Support Their Employees with Burnout

Although I outlined a personal prescription for burnout throughout this book, we must be careful that, when presenting solutions and even describing the landscape, we don't fall into the trap of putting the onus completely on the individual to push change forward.

The collective burnout many have experienced since 2020 has been as much a result of the pandemic as it has been a result of increasingly unsustainable work practices and expectations. In short, this burnout was brewing long before the pandemic, yet a global health crisis sent us over the edge.

The root causes of workplace-induced burnout are deeply rooted and systemic. An individual simply cannot solve systemic issues. However, we can all add to the chorus of voices calling for change. By normalizing conversations on rest and overwork, we can shift paradigms that will eventually shift attitudes that demand shifts in systems.

When it comes to supporting employees through burnout and creating opportunities to foster greater psychological health and well-being, both generally and in the workplace, the United States has some clear opportunities for improvement.

Psychological health and well-being are byproducts of many factors, some of which workplaces have the power to address. Employers can't remove personal triggers that lead to burnout – like the death of a family member, or a cancer diagnosis – but they can move the needle in the many ways work contributes to employee burnout and intersects with our mental health.

Paying employees fair wages, encouraging time off, observing appropriate boundaries, and even in a more drastic sense, moving to remote work or even a four-day work week are all solutions that sound revolutionary on the surface. But they are all doable. I think people are making the biggest calls for their *time* so they have the margin and space to take a beat when life throws the inevitable curveball.

Candid conversations about burnout and mental health in the workplace have evolved tremendously in recent years. There used to be no place for these types of discussions at work. In fact, I personally know people who have worked to hide or mask the fact that they were unable to manage for fear of losing their roles, or have aimed not to give an employer any ammunition for a layoff.

The people who are most vulnerable are generally contending with many factors that can potentially lead to burnout – income insecurity, health disparities, and so on – but they don't always feel that support or a safety net is there.

The pandemic ushered in this global moment where everyone was going through the same thing. The pandemic impacted our mental health and created this unique moment where more people were asking questions, reaching out to therapists, and talking online about stress, depression, and anxiety. It's no wonder calls for workplace policies around paid leave for working parents grew louder. So many people were dealing with the same issues at the same time, and our collective cry was, "This is not sustainable."

So what impacts emotional well-being at work? What contributes to burnout? There's obviously the personal – and that's unique to everyone. But in workplaces it can be traced back to:

- A culture of overwork
- The toxic normalization of putting work first over your family or even your health
- Sustainability. We can see unsustainable practices in personal terms but many workplaces have unsustainable expectations in terms of output: the quality of your relationship with colleagues, your ability to set boundaries around your time, increasing workload, expectations to overwork and do the work of more than one person, lack of support, and the sense that the pace never lets up.

Limitations of the Organization

As I explained in Chapter 12, I encourage folks to explore and develop practices that help them feel more rested and centered and lean into those practices with intention daily. Here are just a few of the practices that are in my personal toolkit, which have been discussed throughout the book:

- Journaling
- Meditation
- Creating a gratitude list
- Prayer
- Breathwork

Just like getting on your Peloton is up to you, it's up to you to integrate regular exercise for your mental health as well.

We can't have a conversation about burnout, psychological health, and well-being without acknowledging the unique challenges of minorities and people of color. There are specific factors that make women, queer people, and people of color more vulnerable to burnout than other groups.

Discrimination based on race, gender, and sexual orientation all take their toll. Additionally, lack of pay equity, housing discrimination, health disparities – as well as the discrimination, lack of equity, and disparities experienced by the people you care about – create another layer of energetic drain on top of the stresses of daily life.

I like to think of it almost like you would think of different conditions when it comes to your physical health. For example, everyone is at risk of catching COVID, the flu, or even the common cold. But you are high risk if you also suffer from asthma or you are immunocompromised because you've been under chemotherapy or some other treatment. Those patients are more vulnerable because of the added issues that come with those comorbidities.

These added pressures that come with issues like dealing with microaggressions and discrimination based on race, gender, and sexual orientation on a daily basis – and in some cases fearing for your personal safety – all create a compounding effect on top of the burnout issues that surface as a result of machine mindset.

Strategies for Companies

Companies can employ various strategies to create a more inclusive and supportive mental health environment for marginalized identities at work:

- Offer opportunities for remote work.
- Offer opportunities for flexible work.
- Allow employees to take regular sabbaticals.
- Implement transparency in hiring and pay and advancement.
- Keep goalposts and performance metrics visible.
- Communicate and compensate in a way that shows you value each employee's contributions.
- Pay fairly across gender, race, and sexual orientation.
- Offer opportunities for professional advancement.
- Encourage rest, breaks, and mental health days.

In short, when employers treat people like machines instead of human beings – and those employees attempt to rise to expectations on that level – burnout is not far behind.

Employees may not be expecting specific benefits around burnout, but access to things like periodic mental health days or company-wide weeks of collective rest certainly are nice. Mainly, I think employees want workplaces to consider the underlying factors that can create that sense of burnout as a byproduct. They want to work where they are:

- Respected
- Considered
- Compensated fairly and equitably
- Given time flexibility
- Given grace for mistakes
- Given time and space to process major life changes like the birth or death of a loved one

Essentially, treat them like human beings. Don't expect the performance of a machine.

How Workplaces Can Support Employees Dealing with Burnout

Employers need to do the work of creating psychological safety and role modeling that it is safe to share their challenges around burnout. But if you're an employee in a workplace that doesn't offer that, proceed with caution.

In terms of communication, if we can normalize symptoms of mental health like we normalize symptoms of physical health, we can be better prepared to have that conversation. So just as you'd first acknowledge that you'd be highly distracted and unproductive at work if you'd just sprained your ankle, no one should expect you to work through the distraction of a major health crisis.

Thinking about our mental health in the same way we view our physical health starts with you normalizing for yourself that everyone has bad days – including you. Your mental health is a part of your overall health. If your overall health is not in a good place, it's okay to communicate that. Secondly, in terms of workplaces that don't create a sense of psychological safety, I don't know that it's necessary for employees to bring up the subject of burnout specifically. If you need to take a sick day, you need to take a sick day. If that sick day is to address your mental health so be it, but if you're not in a situation where you feel that sharing that very personal part of your health is a safe thing to do, then perhaps simply couch it as a sick day.

And even in the cases where psychological safety is not an issue, I think we have to remember that mental health is a part of health, and health is personal. Some people are extremely private about every health challenge and that is fine. Employees don't owe their employers detailed information about health, so employers also need to make allowances for different styles and levels of privacy among individual people.

Company culture always starts at the top, and mental wellness is no exception. When it comes to creating more psychologically healthy cultures at work, leaders play a clear role in role-modeling what these types of conversations can look like and verbalizing that these conversations are welcome.

Companies can do a lot in how they message company culture through company values and what they share about and even the types of programming that they produce. For example, hosting internal conversations about burnout and putting resources behind strategies to work through it communicates that this is a topic a company deems important, this is a topic to which the company wants to give airtime, this is a topic the company is normalizing, and this is not something they will shy away from or stigmatize.

Organizations can open the door by leading first with the type of vulnerability they want to see. Because if it's not authentic, people can sense it. You can't manufacture a sense of safety.

For organizations that are looking to build more trust with the people who work with you, integrity goes a long way. If a person feels as though you care about them, you are a person of integrity, and they can trust you, they are going to be more willing to open up to you and seek your support when they're struggling.

Key Insights

- Machine mindset is starting to crack. We can see this in organizations via successful four-day workweek experiments, wide adoptions of remote work, and weekly paid rest. We can see this with individuals in the rise of wellness retreats and the success of rest-centered enterprises like HURU.
- We want a new model and believe it's possible to have more work-life balance. Existing research points to how our values have shifted toward purposeful lives and work.
- Individuals can't solve systemic problems that lead to burnout, and organizations can't do the individual's personal work of developing a stillness practice.
- People are finding alignment – and rest – with success. Burnout does not have to be an inevitable result of work.

Afterword

For the past few years, a college friend has sent me a dormant amaryllis bulb as a holiday gift each December. The first one she sent a few days before Christmas as a gift for my then tween sons and me on the occasion of my daughter's birth. "I thought you'd enjoy watching something else grow," the card read.

And enjoy we did.

Having never tended a flowering plant indoors during the dead of winter, we didn't know what to expect. But we were quickly wowed by the plant's daily progress. What first appeared only as a brown stump in a pot of dirt soon had a pointed green bud peeking through. We watered, watched, and waited.

And then the miraculous happened. The stem shot up seemingly overnight, and within a few weeks' time, our gift transformed from an unassuming pot of dirt to an enormous display of the most beautiful and vibrant blooms we'd ever witnessed. Just in time for Valentine's Day, the amaryllis put on a show for us. Its brilliant blooms were the payoff of a dormant non-blooming season.

With the pot perched atop our living room mantel, we enjoyed watching the blooms for about 10 days. And then the inevitable happened. The once bright reddish fuchsia flowers began to fade and wilt, dropping petals daily until we decided its blooming was done.

When I researched plant care and what to do next, I was struck by the description I found:

> *"After blooming, the bulb is exhausted and needs time to replenish its depleted food reserves. Amaryllis plants need a period of dormancy* [roughly the same amount of time that elapsed while we were watching the plant grow] *to bloom again."*

After such a breathtaking display of foliage, it only made sense that the plant needed replenishment and rest before it could be expected to bloom again. It would be unreasonable to expect a new, equally brilliant bloom the following week. It would be even more unreasonable to expect a continuous bloom with no wilting or fading over time.

And yet when I think about the modern human approach to blooming, those unreasonable expectations have become the norm. Especially for most Americans, once you hop on the wheel of work, you're expected to steadily improve and stay at your best and most brilliant for the full length of your career. And if you count the achievements that start during elementary school, high school, and college, that's almost a full lifetime of expected blooming. Aside from a handful of government holidays, sick leave, and the vacation days that, according to Pew Research Center, 52% of Americans fail to take full advantage of annually, there is no regular extended period of rest and renewal during the course of one's career.

For parents and caregivers, the expectations only compound. The demands of parenting and caregiving don't end at 6 p.m. and don't skip weekends; they are typically exhaustive unpaid roles many are taking on in addition to their paid labor.

We have unfortunately drifted dangerously far away from the simple principles that govern every other body in nature. How did what would be considered unreasonable for the amaryllis bulb – perpetual full-color blooming – become a normalized expectation for human beings?

Just as the bulb is exhausted and depleted after the hard work of pushing a stem up and forcing flowers to bloom, so too are we. After seasons and seasons of expected blooming, we have reached a tipping point.

We are waking up to the fact that nonstop producing without regular dormant seasons for rest is unsustainable – both for us and for the planet.

It is my hope that this book can be a tool to help you as you detangle from the dangerous expectations of nonstop production that inevitably lead to burnout. I hope that it can support your thinking as you begin to tend to yourself, and prioritize the energy-generating activities and people that give your life meaning and purpose.

Acknowledgments

For Logan, Connor, Leighton, and Marc – thank you for praying for me and championing my inner writer.

For Amber Cabral, for the kickoff and inspiration to go for it.

For all the students of Package Your Genius Academy

For everyone who took time to speak with me for this book – thank you.

About the Author

Amanda Miller Littlejohn is a writer, champion for self-discovery, and executive coach to high achievers. A nationally recognized expert on personal branding and innovator in the public relations space, Littlejohn is the founder of Washington, DC–based leadership and training company Package Your Genius Academy, author of *Package Your Genius: 5 Steps to Build Your Most Powerful Brand*, the *Package Your Genius Personal Branding Companion Workbook*, and host of the podcast by the same name. Through her public speaking for corporate groups, training programs for high-potential talent, and thought leadership advisory for executives, she helps clarify and communicate people's contributions to the world.

Amanda has coached executives at Walmart, Covergirl, EY, Google, Scholastic, Colgate-Palmolive, JP Morgan, Takeda Pharmaceuticals, and Johnson & Johnson, among others. She's presented before employee audiences at Walmart, PayPal, Spotify, AARP, National Science Foundation, and Guardian Life. Truly a global advisor, she enjoys working with independent coaching clients around the globe—from San Francisco to Singapore to Saudi Arabia.

Amanda believes in the power of journaling for self-reflection and regularly shares journaling prompts to help aid in rest, mindfulness, and self-discovery. In her reporting work, she is currently exploring rest, work, burnout, and how Americans are redefining ambition in the post-pandemic era.

An author and journalist, Amanda explores our relationship to work and ambition in the post-pandemic era. Her timely articles on rest and burnout have appeared in the *Washington Post*, the *Huffington Post*, the *Los Angeles Times*, and *Forbes*.

Index